From the Streets of San Francisco

CRACK

The Untold Story

By Rev. Lawrence Gray, Sr.

Second printing

Please visit Rev. Lawrence Gray, Sr's website @
three-pennies.com

or email @
l_gray58@yahoo.com

Softcover 1-4137-6564-5
PUBLISHED BY REV. LAWRENCE GRAY SR.

Printed by DiggyPOD

I dedicate this book to Idris, Natalie, and Lawrence II, thank you for not giving up on your father.

To my brother Clarence: Thank you for pushing me to make this happen (RIP).

To all the suffering addicts out here today, I pray that you surrender your soul to your higher power.

To Angela; thank you for helping to save my life.

Acknowledgements

I acknowledge and thank God for keeping me and allowing me the chance to help someone else by the blood of Jesus Christ.

Thank you, Mom and Dad, for putting up with a prodigal son who finally came home.

Thank you, Vickie and Charles, for allowing me to type on your computer many a night trying to complete this project.

Very special thanks to all the people who contributed their stories to make this vision real.

To my wife, Diane, thank you for helping me and giving me the chance to be your husband.

To Brittany Luddington: Who would have thought we would have come this far after a chance meeting (pre edit).

To Nick Chavez: Thank you for being you and drawing the book cover.

To Loretta: If it were not for you, the birth of this story would have never come into being.

God Bless you all!

Book Review

Despite rough edges, "Crack" succeeds with brutal honesty

Some books are very tough to read. Not because of the way they are written, but because of their content.

That's the case with the Rev. Lawrence Gray Sr.'s book, "From the Streets of San Francisco: Crack, The Untold Story."

Told the from the point of view of the crack addict, this book pulls no punches. It is dark and rough around the edges, like the people within who tell their tragic stories.

This is not a medical treatise on addiction, nor is it a how-to guide to getting clean. While Gray and his fellow addicts credit finding God—or a "higher power," as Gray calls it many a time—and hard work in getting themselves clean, they can only offer experience, not medical advice, in the battle.

Gray, who works today as a North Pole preacher, believes in getting right to the point. The first line of the book, in the Introduction, is hard-hitting and tells the reader where the book is heading: "I am absolutely 100 percent guilty; guilty of the crime of being a drug addict ..."

There's no way you can think this is going to be an easy read or have a fairytale plot or ending. It also grabs your attention, and makes you want to read further.

He calls the addiction a substitute for God, and continues: "I let that sub sit in the classroom of my mind, heart and soul taking control of the most formative years of my adult life; years that are wasted: time that can never come again."

I was intrigued. And it kept me wading through what are some serious editing errors—or rather, a lack of editing. Misspellings, incorrect grammar, run-on sentences—slogging through was almost impossible. It is very difficult—for me, anyway—to concentrate on content when presentation is poor.

But I began to realize that the poor grammar and bad English was central to the story Gray is telling. These addicts tell their stories in their own words—grimy, sloppy, in fits and starts, incorrect and uneducated. And it begins to add a depth to the message that polished prose would not have. It puts the readers inside the heads and hearts and souls of the tellers, brings us closer to them, allows us to feel some of their agony as they recall their years of wallowing in the depths of addiction, doing anything and hurting anyone in order to feed that hunger.

It's a powerful book in that respect.

Gray uses some great imagery in his description of addiction. He calls crack "Satan's cronie," and tells of the "Jekyll and Hyde" transformations that come over the user as they start their journey down the road.

And while the idea of drugs as a demon and God as the demon slayer isn't original, it works especially well here, perhaps because of the "Reverend" before Gray's name.

"When you're using dope ain't nothing weird."

I thought it was hyperbole at first, since I've never experienced any type of addiction. But as I got further into the book and met some of the addicts telling their stories, I began to see that Gray was right. Nothing these people saw or did or experienced seemed odd to them—even the woman whose baby was stillborn, with his brain on the outside of his skull. She just went home and smoked some more crack to get over it.

Then there's John, who started smoking pot. "Marijuana became my God and I worshiped the herbal plant of green."

John talks of his descent with gripping intensity: How he became a criminal to support his habit, living in the Tenderloin area of San Francisco, where "lions" preyed on the weak.

"They would devour you if given the chance with fangs of blood dripping from their eyes of death." The mixed metaphors actually tell more of a story than one would think, and give a good picture of the confusion that typifies an addict's thinking.

John also brings up the paradox of addiction: That sooner or later, what once felt good becomes agonizing. "It came to a point where getting high was not fun for me anymore, getting high was not all that I thought it was. Getting high had caused me misery."

In fact, that's a common statement throughout the book: Most addicts take the road to salvation because it's no longer "fun" to be high.

Not all crack addicts are sleazy lowlifes with bad childhoods. Many of Gray's storytellers come from decent backgrounds. More than one grew up as a military dependent. And many tried to maintain an outward appearance of stability and uprightness even during their addiction, being what Gray calls a "functional addict."

Wanda tells about the dilemma of knowing—in your sober moments—that addiction is killing you, but being unable to change.

"Although in the back of your mind you really want to do the right things and you want to live right and take care of your business like you are supposed to but the psychological effect of crack has you turned inside out and you just don't care. All you live for is another hit of crack."

This book tells of vanished families, criminal behavior, prison stays, degradation, lost money, time and health. It is, as I said earlier, not an easy book to read. It is gritty, dirty, pathetic and hard to take. It leaves the reader emotionally wrung out, feeling torn between pity for the addicts and anger that they allowed themselves to fall into the pit.

And there's admiration that they pulled themselves out of the pit.

It also reminds the reader—and the addicts themselves—that the war is never really won. They win daily battles in staying clean and sober, but each knows that it's a short slide down into the pit again.

And as hard as it is to read, as hard as it is to take, it is also disarmingly, brutally honest. It's real. It's truth.

And those of us who haven't fallen into the pit, who think we're strong enough that we'd never be one of the chapters in this book, it makes us realize that it's just a thin, fragile line between us and them.

Libbie Martin
is a copy editor for the Fairbanks Daily News-Miner and a freelance writer. She lives in Fairbanks.

Table of Contents

INTRODUCTION

I AM ABSOLUTELY 100% GUILTY; GUILTY of the crime of being a drug addict, addicted to crack; guilty of the crime of letting another substitute the Christ-like, the God in me. For many years I let that sub sit in the classroom of my mind, heart and soul taking control of the most formative years of my adult life; years that are wasted: time that can never come again. Time which there is no looking back to correct the wrong to right, to live and to love taking the cornerstone of life and thus being the tallest of any building, mountain or sky; time. The beauty of it all is that now those mountains exist, those buildings are me and the sky is mine. The fallacies of crack are so bewildering, so baffling, beholding, bedazzling and ever so bewitching. What you must understand; no what you don't understand is why unless you have been there before. Well not to worry, you are not alone. The thing is this, you will never know and those who think they know—don't. For those who are fortunate to have equilibrium enough to balance wisdom and understanding to know that there is a way, and the way is God; seek him now.

Crack is Satan's chorine who does the work he doesn't have

to because once you draft him into your ranks, you're nothing but a foot soldier, standing point on the terrain of your life and as hunters would say: "It's open season." Yes, my claim to fame was letting crack take my heart, soul, mind and spirit dwelling on damnation. Enough is enough, I told myself finally, and I am not having it; that is what I told myself time and time again yet succumbing to its magic, but the quicker than eye motion moved once too many times making me decide whether to quit or die. I decided not to die; what about you; not me, not like that.

Addiction to crack is raising destruction, misery and pain so high that the Dow Jones market chasers might compare its value three times as that of gold. Crack, what is it? Crack has many a fool; crack no time for school. Crack knows no wrong; no right. Crack next to God all natural the ultimate chemical high. Crack; what about it? Crack; what is it? Tell me what, oh what can crack do? It depletes your health, causing you to lose weight drastically, taking the calcium from your bones. It takes all your wealth and anything else you have of materialistic value. It changes your personality making you become a Dr. Jekyll and Mr. Hyde in its truest form having very little or no ethics, none at all, no respect, no regard or consideration for anyone except yourself and another hit to get high. It will make you do things you thought you would never do; lie, steal, cheat, deceive, swindle, defraud and con people, especially your loved ones; giving you a false security that is totally beyond the realm of reality and yet knowing all this you do time after time, after time, again and again and again.

What is this substance that can do all these things? What is this demon burning deep down in my soul making me do all these things I do not want to do? It's a drug called crack; a form of cocaine derived from hydrochloride that has been chemically treated from the salt of cocaine. It is then crystallized into a white or yellow rock that you smoke in a glass pipe, a jar, a modified radio antenna, aluminum foil or anything else that one can use as a smokeable inhaler. Its addiction is so overwhelming, so powerful that nothing else in life matters at all, absolutely nothing; except having some more and more and more.

10

If you have never subjected yourself to be under its influence—good, great, super, magnificent and any other positive word that you can think of, don't; for if you do so happen to make the fatal mistake where there is no turning back and indulge trying it, tempting the hand of fate, make no doubt about it you will become one of the thousands, millions of people who are already slaves, hooked, junkies on the rock. One might think he or she can handle and enjoy the euphoric high of crack with its everlasting addiction, wrong; think again. It starts out that way but, believe you me, the rock will take full control and precedence in your life; over, around and through you as you will never know. Some people come out of it and back to the reality of life by the grace of God but many, I am sad to say without any reservation, do not and many have even lost their lives.

Beyond these pages are stories of everyday people who have in their lifetime become preys, slaves to the rock (crack cocaine); beholding to its master's whip; cutting and stripping, bleeding to the depths of no escape within their mind. Read these stories and understand why you don't want to be a crackhead. They are true unadulterated and unaltered, given to me in the form of their individual thinking while being held in bondage through the captivity of their addiction. Read these stories with an open mind; so open that you become transfigured and transformed into the monster they once were and be sure to let your children read them because they need to know the reality of this drug called crack; then read them again and again so that they may stay ingrained upon your mind as well as theirs; so that you won't make the vital mistake in life and become a junkie, a crackhead.

For those of you who are still hooked and really, really want to quit, you too read this book and in between the pages with God on your side, you might find a way out of your diseased mind causing this terrible addiction. It is up to you to make that decision. I pray that you do before it's too late.

You would think that I have taken leave of my senses when I tell you that this drug called crack is so domineering, so imperative, so imperious and so powerful that it will make an

11

individual do things they thought they would never ever do in life totally against your moral virtuous standards and beliefs; such as stealing, robbery, forgery, embezzlement, prostitution, just to name a few of the illegal and immoral sins and or deeds that a person may do to support their addiction; oh yes! Let us not forget the ultimate sin: murder; to take another person's life just for the pleasure of smoking some more crack. When I say the "more," it is because at this stage of the high in its demonic form a person resulting to murdering another human being has definitely been smoking crack for a long period of time; many hours and days in and out. Then again it depends on their mind whether or not they are stable, only that person can determine that. However, if you continuously hit the pipe you are crossing over the line of sanity.

I hope and trust that this book will make you so aware that you dare not even attempt to yield into temptation. I hope that it frightens you enough to tremble at the thought of ever using any drug that will inevitably control your mind; those who have never used to not ever use. Almost, and then again may be not, everyone knows of someone, be it family or friend or foe, who is hooked but no one seems to know what to do to combat it. Read this book and maybe you will find the answer and if not, you will definitely understand it more than you ever have before and that's a promise.

What many people fail to see and comprehend out of their own ignorance in regards to this subject is that smoking crack is like no other high in the world. There is no comparison to alcohol, marijuana or any other illegal drug, except heroin, why? Because there is *never, never, never,* let me say this one more time this "never ever eeenough."

When and whoever came up with the saying that "one is too many and a thousand is not enough" definitely was speaking of crack cocaine and the weirdest aspect of it all is that it is all psychological; all in your mind and this is no joke. Unlike a person being addicted to heroin which consumes the bloodstream of your body with its own powerful addiction, making it necessary for you to have more in order not to be sick, not to hurt with pain, like a case of a real bad flu which requires a dose of medication to subdue the pain. Crack, on the other hand, is all a mental thing. Now, comparing the two you would think it would be easy not to do crack; surprise, it isn't.

PROLOGUE

CRACK COCAINE IS SO WIDESPREAD, LIKE a grassfire out of control, and as you know when some grassfires are out of control the only thing that the firefighters can do is let it burn itself out and that's exactly what is happening with the epidemic use of crack. It is so out of control that the only solution is to let it burn out but while it's burning it is also taking lives with it. Lives of people who could be prosperous and living well and just the like the grassfire that kills and destroys acres of land and its inhabitants therein, meaning the family, crack is doing the same thing with human lives. People's lives who are in prison, people's lives who are dealers and peoples lives who are robbers, stealers, whoremongers, fornicators, homosexual and bisexual alike, totally obliterated from the true form of life, the natural real human being.

So, what is the solution? Only the person who is strung out can answer that question but then again you may not know. If you want my answer, the only answer is God, Jehovah, Allah, Buddha or whomever you recognize as God or your Higher Power as you have come to recognize it.

15

Just how could something that makes you feel so good be totally wrong, easy; it's Satan, believe it or not, I do know that. I've been there before and don't want to go there anymore. I am not going to go there anymore as long as I stay surrendered to my Higher Power, Jesus Christ. I'm not trying to convert you; I'm just passing the message on, Jesus Saves; but you figure it out, even if you have all the money that you ever wanted, you still cannot and will never conquer the addiction of crack cocaine, just like the celebrities, politicians, and high-priced entertainers who do have the money, a lot of money more money than many of us will ever have, they cannot even with all their revenue conquer the addiction to crack. Why? Why? Why? Simple, because there is never enough, you always want more and more and more; until you finally pass out from exhaustion, some having to force themselves to eat in order to just have strength enough to keep on living for another hit of that crack cocaine and this is only momentarily because after you eat and rest, you're back at it again until the next time fatigue sets in.

Blame it on the government, blame it on Big Brother, the communist, the mafia, the militia or whomever you want to blame it on; it really doesn't matter. What matters is this; you can't smoke the rock unless you pick up the rock, it's that simple. It's there and it is going to always be there and if you get hooked or if you stay hooked it is no one else's fault except your own. Some people want to come out of it, others don't. If you do want to quit with all your heart, mind and soul, then perhaps you can find something within these pages to help you because it's all here in black and white and all you have to do is pick it up, practice it and use it. Most of all you have to surrender because you are totally powerless by far.

Let me say one more thing before you illicit to read this book; there are a lot of young men and women selling crack or other drugs thinking that this is road to financial success; for some it is but it's only a matter of time before the "pie in the sky" dream catches up with them. It is also a road that leads to looking over your shoulder all the time for the police, dope fiends who want to rip you off, people setting you up but most of all, it's a road that will lead to prison and sometimes death.

It's hard for some young people or even older to resist the temptation of making money so easy but if they (the dealers) do not have anyone to distribute to do their business, it will fold. That is highly unlikely because as long as there is crack there will be someone to sell it to. Only you, the user, can do this; you who are strung out, you who are weak, it's time to get strong and quit; quit now before it is too late.

LAWRENCE

LET'S SEE WHEN AND WHERE DID it all begin; it seems so long ago that I was standing in back of the school gym, sniffing glue. I was thirteen years old at the time and had just embarked upon my chemical substance abuse in my life, little did I know at that time that I would become a full-fledged junkie. I started smoking weed and drinking wine; Ripple (Pagan Pink) was my favorite, Boonesfarm and Annie Green Springs. Marijuana did not do too much for me at first but as I increased my daily use I began to feel the sensation of being high. Me and my friends would get high everyday; cutting classes, going out stealing merchandise from stores, cars and businesses in the neighborhood. Oh did we have a field day before taxes ran the businesses out of San Francisco. Every day before and after school we would stop off at these businesses and steal; there were companies like Nabisco, Kraft Foods, Planters Peanut, 7up, Blue Seal and Langendorf Bakeries, The Mobile Catering Trucks, Gallo Salami, Laura Scurdders Potato Chip Company and many administrative businesses, warehouses and supermarkets. By the time we would get to school we had so much stuff it was unreal.

19

I never broke into people's homes, some of my friends did but that seemed to be a taboo and it just did not jell with me.

The birth of the Haight Ashbury District in San Francisco was high within itself, the Hippie Era, Love Peace and Happiness; Turn on, Tune in and Drop Out and get high; man that was so cool. The hippies were so right on that you did not even need any money to get high, just walk down the district and people would turn you on and if you did spend money you got more than your proper due.

I became a member of a singing group (The Philosophics). Man we were the baddest local group in the city and it's something about being an entertainer in the secular world. During this time entertaining, drugs and parties went hand in hand. You stay up all night or most of the night partying and you needed a little something to keep you going, a joint, some coke, a bennie, black beauty (pills) and, of course, alcohol, anything to keep up with the pace. I started snorting cocaine when I was about eighteen, it was a beautiful feeling, one that I would not let go of for many years; snorting cocaine and smoking weed, drinking cognac—that was the life and I definitely can't forget the parties and the women; oh what a time, all night long; night after night.

During this time I also had a job working construction and me and my partners in crime got our first paycheck and decided to all pitch in and buy some dope, cocaine. I remember, it was seven of us and we had spent about fifty dollars each on some coke. I was snorting mine from an album cover, a standard procedure but everyone else in the room was rolling their sleeves up to bang it, (shoot it intravenously).

I asked one of the dudes, Smitty, how did shooting dope make you feel. He was releasing the tie from his arm and his eyes opened real wide and he said to me with the most intense look on his face: "Lawrence, I don't think you wan to try this."

"Why?" I asked.

"It's too good and you will get hooked."

"Come on, man," Red said.

"I'll fix you up."

20

I said OK and at that moment Henry, Red's brother, stood up over me and hit me square in the face knocking me on the bed, and said, "Man, don't you ever shoot no dope as long as you live." Then he turned to Red and said, "Don't try to turn that boy out."

You see, I came up in a Christian home and friends respected the authority of my mother and father. I was literally raised in church in God with good values and I know that because of those roots instilled in me is why I am clean today. I was thankful for Henry that day because I learned that shooting dope was the ultimate high and that if you tried it you would definitely get hooked.

Years passed and my addiction to cocaine and smoking weed was getting the best of me but I still maintained my job and my responsibilities. I was a functional addict. I was snorting cocaine so much and so often that my nose would bleed and the antinodes became so sore that my nose would hurt as if someone was sticking needles in my nostrils; that was a hurting feeling. By this time I was married to my wife Loretta and she was not aware of my drug use. We had two kids, Natalie and Lawrence II. I had an older son, Idris, from Verdia; she was a real good mother. She would let Idris come over and stay with us all the time and none of them were aware of my drug use; that's the thing about being an addict you try to hide it from other people, especially your loved ones but eventually what's in the dark comes to the light.

I woke up one morning and my nose was killing me; it was bleeding. I called my cousin Bobby; he was my drug supplier and I was telling him how my nose was paining me. He gave me a solution because he had experienced the same thing. The solution he gave me haunted and stayed with me for 13 years, to the day my baby was born, August 1986.

At the time it was called freebase, the purest form of cocaine you could ever encounter next to shooting it. I remember sitting in his house and him putting the rock on the screen; inhaling it, trying to feel the effect of the dope. I got sprung about the third time I hit it; man what a feeling. It was so good, I wanted some

21

more thus becoming a crackhead but little did I know at the time. I was working the graveyard shift as a computer operator, I learned this skill as well as others while in high school and on-the-job training. We had a class in high school called office machines and I was drawn to the machines, they fascinated me, learning to operate them at a rapid, accurate speed and I was good at it being one of the fastest typists, keypunch operator, better now known as keying, and any other machine that was in my class. I was tops; as a matter of fact, it was only class I ever received an "A" as a grade in high school.

Anyway, I started smoking crack every day and it was good for about a year or so. Every payday I would spend at least half of my check on cocaine, three hundred dollars a week. To compensate spending my paycheck so that my wife would not find out, I would steal. You see, by me knowing my office skills and how to steal enabled me to get good jobs in a lot of offices downtown in San Francisco; banks, insurance companies and businesses like that and there was always something of value around to steal, always. My habit was starting to get bad. My wife and I moved out of our dwelling in Pacifca to live with her sister and her husband in South San Francisco in order to save money; hell, that's when things got out of control, because instead of saving the money that I was supposed to be saving, I was spending it all on crack.

My habit was so bad that when I went to work at night in San Mateo, about fifteen miles from home, I would get to work and start my machines and go find an empty office, break out my crack pipe and commence getting high. This went on night after night. Man, I was really starting to become a walking nightmare but you would have never known it by looking at me because I camouflaged myself pretty damn good.

I began to run out of money and started looking for something to steal, searching each office for anything of value; then it occurred to me that you can recycle computer paper at the paper mill in San Francisco and this job that I was working on had a lot of computer paper. So, I would fill up my car—I drove

Datsun at the time—the back and the front seat as well as the trunk with boxes of brand-new computer paper; I would get off work, drive to the paper mill in the morning and cash it in. Most of the time all that paper I stole did not amount to much at the mill. The most I ever got was $40 for about 20 boxes of paper but that was enough at the time in order to get high. This went on for about a year. Then one night I was searching the offices, looking for something to steal, and discovered the petty cash box. Man, was I happy because I knew I could buy some crack. I took about $100 the first night; then I took about $60 the second night and on the third night I went to the office to get some more cash and lo and behold it wasn't there. I began to search all over in desperation. I finally found it and this time I took all of the money.

I never got caught but the people at work suspected it was me; they just could not prove it. My work performance was really starting to deteriorate. I would come to work late or not at all depending on how I felt because I would be up all day and night smoking crack. Then one day my boss called me at home and told me that I was fired. I was pissed off; the nerve of myself at the time to get angry with the boss for firing me for not coming to work. Smoking crack makes a person wig out. So, that night, at about twelve o'clock, I got into my car; drove to the job I had been terminated from; used my card key and went into the warehouse and got some more computer paper for the last time; cashed it in and got some more dope.

My addiction was taking full control at this point in my life and I kept trying to keep it in prospective but that was far-fetched. I got another job working at a bank, 1st Nationwide, in the administrative office as an office assistant and continued my daily use, or as often as I could, of getting high. My wife by this time was aware of my drug addiction and tried to stand by me as much as she could, enduring a lot of pain along the way and I'm sorry that I ever brought drugs into my home because it destroyed my family and my life. The job at the bank did not pay me enough money to support my high; so I started looking for a better job with higher pay so that I get higher. I found it at a freight shipping and leasing company downtown in San Francisco as a telex/fax operator. It lasted for about two years before I had to give my resignation because of an incident that occurred while I was there. It was the 1990 NFL football playoffs; I was living in Vacaville at the time with my family living in a nice home which we were leasing with the option to buy—this was about an hour commute east of San Francisco.

Anyway, I had collected about $200 and decided I would go and buy some dope at lunchtime so that I could get high when I got off work. I caught the bus, the 15/3rd & Kearney and headed for the hood to buy some dope. While I was riding the bus, I ran into Smitty and he said that he was going to pick up his car at his mother's house and that he knew where we could buy some crack and we did.

We went back to his mother's house so that we could take a hit before he took me back to work. We went downstairs and started getting high and time began to pass. It was getting pretty close to one o'clock and he said: "It's time for you to go back to work." I said, "OK, just one more hit." Hell, I never did make it back to work. I did not even make it home that night. We ended up smoking crack all night. I spent all the money I had collected for the football pool.

Now, I'm trying to figure out in my mind exactly what I was going to do to keep my job and pay those people back. So, the next day I went to my boss and confessed and told him that I had a chemical substance abuse problem and asked if he could help me. In essence, all I was doing was trying to save my job and my wife from leaving me. It worked; I paid the money back that I had collected for the football pool from my paycheck and the job put me in a rehabilitation program in Sacramento. I stayed for thirty days and I learned about substance abuse. I learned that it was a sickness, a disease of the mind and body. It did not do me too much good because as soon as I got out, I went and bought some more crack. I was not ready to surrender.

As a matter of fact, the first weekend I was there I wanted to go home. The counselors (four of them surrounded me) and said it was my drug calling me and I said: "Bull, I'm getting out of here." I wanted an Out-Patient Program and they would not give it to me and I figured the only reason they did this was to get as much revenue as they could from my insurance.

Anyway, I went home that weekend and bought some crack on Saturday night. I stayed out all night smoking at a friend's house. (In actuality you have no friends if you are a dope fiend because the friend you do have will turn on you for dope in a heartbeat). I wanted some more dope. Man, it's never enough dope once you start smoking, there's never enough. So at about two o'clock that morning I drove to a spot where I knew I could cop some more dope and the dude burnt me; he took my money and lied, saying that he gave it to the dealer and that we had to wait till he got back from going to buy it.

I finally figured out what had happened, went to my trunk to get my bumper jack because I was getting ready to mess him up real bad. As I was in my trunk the police drove up. I tossed the jack and they ran a warrant check on me. I had an outstanding parking ticket. They took me to jail; released me later on that night and gave me citation to appear in court at a later date. When I got home, I had my wife take me back to the rehabilitation program because I knew at that time I had a serious problem but I still was not ready to give it up. I was in denial.

Well, I went back to work after completing the program and lasted there for about another three months before I got caught in a dead heat trying to steal the petty cash box, I turned in my resignation, left, and went to my mother's house. I told her I had been fired for bad attendance and she looked at me and knew it was a lie; there's always something about your mother and you just can't hide. I began to reflect on the time that I burnt my mother and father. It was really sad. Damn, it's hard telling this but you people need to know the truth about the addiction to crack and its overwhelming power that seizes your mind when you are hooked.

My wife had just had our son at U.C. Hospital. I left the

hospital to go steal a camera from Sears, got some film, took pictures of the birth of our son, went and traded that camera for dope and got high. While my wife was in the hospital recuperating from the birth or son, I got paid from my job and spent my whole entire check at my friend's house smoking dope, all night long.

I smoked so much dope my heart started beating real fast and I went and checked myself into Kaiser Hospital. The nurse asked me what I had been doing after taking my vitals and I said: "Nothing." She said that my pulse rate and blood pressure were up way beyond normal. They put me in the "Blue Room" because at the time I was on the verge of having a heart attack. I went home about four hours later; lay down and promised myself that I would never smoke again.

Now, my money is all spent and my wife is at her mother's with our newborn son, expecting me to show up with money. I called my mother and told her I had been abducted by some drug dealers whom I owed money to and that they were going to kill me if I did not pay them. She became very excited and sympathetic towards my ordeal. She gave me the money, ($500) her and my father, and that was one of the worst feelings I had; burning my parents because of my addiction but I could not go to my wife with no money or else I would have caught hell from her. So, I did what I had to do and at that time even though I felt bad about it, I knew it had to be done because I was a crack addict.

That's something about being addicted to crack; you do things that are so crazy and you know it's crazy but you do it anyway in the name of crack just to get another hit. This was the most despicable deed I had ever done during my addiction. I felt like a dog but I did it anyway. I broke my crack pipe, fell on my knees and started praying and crying to the Lord to help me and that lasted for about a day. I got another pipe and kept getting high.

I lost the lease with the option to buy our house in Vacaville because I did not exercise my two-year window of opportunity until the last two months of the option and I had the money to do so in that period but I was stuck on stupid. My wife had retired from her job at Pacific Bell and between me and Uncle Sam stealing her money, she had none left. We lost the house and that too was a very regrettable incident in my life. Once again I cried and cried and kept getting high and high and high. I was messed up and at this point in my life I had a death wish. I started doing things, crazy things and didn't care. I would go to the supermarkets and steal as if I owned the store and I was a good thief. I specialized in stealing meat and pharmaceutical products because everybody had to eat and everybody sooner or later got sick. I still would work on temporary job assignments, trying to make ends meet and my wife was still in my corner but the end was drawing near.

Man, I used to go to the drug dealers and take orders to steal what they wanted; come back and get my dope. I started getting so paranoid every time I smoked crack; walking around with a knife in my hand (in my own house) looking out windows, putting chairs against the doors, hearing people talking waiting to break in my house. Man, I was insane. I remember once my wife went to visit her mother in Fairfield—her and the kids—and I was smoking dope and hearing things. I thought someone was trying to come in to kill me. It was so real it was more than scary; it was a nightmare. I lay down in the bed but not before putting every kind of obstacle I could leading to my bedroom door so that I could hear the people when they came down the hall: newspapers, plants, toys, shoes, balls, chairs—lying down with the knife in my hand waiting to kill anything that moved. I was so paranoid from smoking crack, I started crying and praying, crying and praying to God please, please deliver me, please help to let this go. Then I would come down and I would start the whole thing all over again and again and again.

After losing our home in Vacaville and living with my wife's mother for about a year, we finally moved to Vallejo. I started working at the school district and things were going pretty well at first. But I kept getting high and things will never go well once you're an addict and you do not admit and submit yourself to the

Lord and I knew this but I kept on keeping on and being forewarned by my wife that this was the last time and that she could not take it anymore and that if I messed up again she was leaving.

Well, anyway, while I was working in the office, I started stealing money from the school district. There was always money around in the office and I felt as if I had walked into a mini bank enabling me to get money and anything else of value to trade for dope. I was a substitute administrative clerk; so therefore I would go from school to school as they needed my services and each school I went to I stole money or something of value.

While working at this one school, I noticed that the kids were selling candy to raise money for some kind of school project. I watched the secretary collect the money envelopes and put them in the safe in a bigger envelope. Waiting for the right opportunity, I went into that safe and at first I would just take one or two money envelopes that the kids had turned in. Then one day I took the whole big envelope. I think I had about nine hundred dollars. I gave my wife some money and she said, "Where did you get this money." I told her, "Don't worry about it." I thought about what I heard a preacher say one day; "The devil might have brought it but God sent it." Hell, if she had known the truth she would have been scared to death; after all, I did lead a life of deception and sin and was sinking oh so, so fast.

I am almost at the end of my rope (actually I was at the end; dangling). I am at the point where caring was totally obsolete and any way I could get money I was going to get it by hook or crook. I remember my uncle, who has passed away years ago; he too was hooked on dope, heroin. He ended up on the dialysis machine because he lost both of his kidneys. Well, I remember him telling me one day that anything you take in this world, the white man's world, is yours because he stole everything he got from somebody else and when you see something in the store or anywhere and it belongs to him, it belongs to you and I kind of used his saying along the way in life to justify my illicit behavior of breaking the law and my shortcomings knowing though in the realness of my mind that "Thou shalt not steal" was a commandment of God which I ignored completely. I was totally transformed into a madman seeking to get high every waking moment of my life.

My family suffered tremendously. I ignored my responsibilities at home; my wife was starting to literally hate me and my children were torn inside themselves because they knew something was wrong with their father and that their lives were unhappy. I had already begun taking things out of the house selling them for drugs: my wife's jewelry, the children's video games, movies, and anything of material value that was not strapped down I took and traded for crack. I am absolutely insane at this time but I still managed to keep my job at the school district but soon lost it. I got caught taking twenty dollars from the change jar and the ironic part of it was that I did it right in front of the lady's face, the principal of the school. You see, she asked me to give her change from this jar full of paper money and since I already was a suspect or so I thought in the missing money syndrome from the school safe, I did not feel good about that money that was sitting in my face. I figured that they were trying to set me up but in actuality it was the paranoia imbedded in my mind from smoking crack for so long a period of time.

Anyway, I go to make change for a five-dollar bill and notice that there was a twenty in the jar and while I was putting the money back in the jar, I put the twenty-dollar bill in the palm of my hand and transferred it to my pocket thinking that my hand was quicker than her eye. Later on that afternoon she called me into her office and told me what she had seen, and she could not believe what I had done especially right in front of her face and as a result of that I was terminated, once again.

I went home and told my wife I had been laid off and that they would call me when the workload picked up. She was very skeptical with my story and told me that if I did not get it together real soon she was leaving.

Now, I am without a job again and the rent is due. My wife is doing childcare and it is not enough to keep us together financially. I started calling on my partners in crime and ran a check scam, which entailed me buying merchandise at this particular store with bogus checks and then taking the merchandise back and getting the cash for it. I would have to give a third of what I got but that was cool with me. I think I made about three thousand dollars in two months and it kept things in check at home until I did not have any more money. Still, I'm getting high every day smoking crack.

I used to come home and walk straight past my family in the living room while they were all watching television and go straight to the bathroom, sit on the toilet seat smoking crack and being paranoid while doing so, and when I ran out and came down a little from being paranoid, I would go to the supermarkets and steal meat. I remember this one incident when I went to Lucky's Supermarket to steal some meat and there was always this one guy, who used to bag groceries and he knew my game, and every time I came into the store he would watch and follow me. Well, this one particular occasion I went into the store and he was not there; man, I felt relieved. So, I go to the meat department to steal some meat. I picked up four packs of filet mignon (I always stole the most expensive meat). I started walking down another aisle so that I could put them in my pants and walk out and lo and behold when I got to aisle and turned down the lane there he was; the bagger. I was so bold and crazy that I walked right up to him and said: "What is your problem, I'm trying to get my hustle on and this should mean nothing to you because you don't own this store."

He said, "Put it back."

So, I started walking back to the meat department, then I thought, *The hell with this.* I turned around and said. "I'm taking this meat and you ain't gonna do a thing about it."

I started walking towards the door. He called for some help from the other checkers and as they approached me, I picked up a bottle of Cappuccino and started swinging at them and they let me go. I walked out got into my car, looked in the mirror at myself and said: "You are really sick, dude." Turned on the ignition, drove off and traded those steaks for crack; now this I knew was lunacy without a doubt.

Here I am going crazy stuck on stupid and did not care. I had this death wish breathing down my back in the hallways of my mind, wishing something would happen to me to make me stop even if it meant death; I was ready to die; tired of being and living like an animal, a vulture, scavenging for scraps of life, tired of going nowhere fast. It seemed to me that death was the most peaceful way out of this hellhole in the darkness of my mind and that with death I would not have any problems; with death no more issues, with death no more responsibilities, with death freedom from the light within. I did not care anymore.

A couple of days later, I got up one morning and went to Safeway to steal some more meat and my thought this time was to make a big sting. So, I went to the back of the store pretending I needed some boxes for moving; at least that's what I told the lady. I got the boxes and came back to the aisle where I had already stashed about $300 worth of meat; beef, and chicken in a shopping cart. As I was putting the meat from the shopping cart into the boxes this lady came down the aisle, the same one who had given me the boxes and she said: "You can't do this." I was angry not because she caught me but that she had seen through my façade. I said: "Yeah, OK," but I was pissed off and I stayed right there putting the meat in the boxes. It was crazy but that's what I did. She went to get someone and when she left, I just left the meat there and headed toward the door. I was stopped by some male employees, I think it was two or three right outside the store and I figured they couldn't do anything to me especially since I did not have anything in my possession. I forgot I had put two big candy bars in my pockets for the kids.

As I started walking towards the car, they somewhat surrounded me and asked me to come back into the store. I said "screw you" and went to my pocket to pull out my knife and thought they couldn't do anything because I didn't have anything but I did; I just forgot. They called the police and I was taken to jail for petty theft.

31

Now, I'm sitting in jail; the year is 1994 and I'm starting to think about what the hell I have been doing all these years and start to once again cry and pray. I prayed and I prayed talking to God pleading with him to deliver me from the body of death that I was living in; to take away my desire of crack and cure my diseased mind. I was so depressed at times I thought about taking my own life but I kept on praying and praying, crying to my wife on the phone telling her that this was all behind me and she said she had enough.

I spent three days in jail; got out on a Thursday, went home and fell on my knees and started praying again, crying and pleading to my family, all of them, telling them that I had a drug addiction problem and that I have truly turned my life over to Jesus and whatever the consequences that I have to go through, whatever I have to suffer to make things right that I was willing to do.

Now, mind you, we are going to be evicted the following week because the rent is past due. I went to court trying to buy some time but the judge wasn't hearing it. One of my partners in crime called me and told me it was on; a job we had been planning for about a month. The job was to rob a bank; a holdup. He had a teller at this particular bank and all I had to do while he would drive was to go on this particular Saturday, take him a note and he was going to give us $25,000; I mean, it was a piece of cake because we had an inside man who also was a functional crack addict. I told him I wasn't going to do it. I said: "I'm tired of living this life that I've been living." I further told him: "I'm going to walk the straight and the narrow as best as I can with the Lord." My wife was listening to my conversation at this time because normally during these types of calls I would take the phone in my bedroom and talk but I let her hear this so that she would know that I was for real.

Normally, in my cracked out mind I would have jumped on this illegal job opportunity but I knew I was headed for prison or the graveyard and enough had become enough. It wasn't fun anymore. I could not remember the last time when getting high was fun. It was an addiction. This crack had me insane. Satan was in full control and I had enough of this life and this time I truly surrendered my addiction to the Lord.

Well, as a result of me not pulling off the bank job, we got evicted. I kept to my word that I was going to walk the straight and narrow and whatever God had in store for me I had to go through it. My wife left along with the children and I went to my mother's house in San Francisco. Now, my life has been on the right track by the grace and mercy of my heavenly Father. I have been clean now for five years and I know that it's only the grace of God that is keeping me alive today but I have to admit that I did relapse because of losing my wife. I stole the meat from my parents' freezer and I used it as an excuse to escape reality to get high and smoke some more crack.

The road has not been easy this past year. I still have conflicting emotions in terms of trying to rekindle my relationship with my wife and my family. It has been a bumpy and rough road but I am not fretting nor worried anymore. I am taking it one day at a time. Trying to win back the love and respect for the whole family has not been easy but people are starting to believe in me again. It's so hard for people to believe in you after you've burnt them so many times for so long (meaning my loved ones). They are scared that it will happen again and I understand that and I have to dance to the music and keep on living. God's knows my heart and I pray for his guidance every day, sometimes every moment and he gives me the strength to carry on.

Today I have a permanent job making pretty good money. I'm in the process of paying my back taxes, child support and getting my driver's license again. Ain't that a trip; not even having a valid license. You don't think about things like that when you are addicted to crack; at least I didn't because on the road of addiction these simple matters of doing the right thing mattered nothing at all to me. I thank God from the depth of my heart and soul for delivering me and I pray for the forgiveness of all the wronged that I have done and I know people don't forgive too easy but I am dealing with it.

I have always had this idea in the back of mind to write this book but I knew I could never do it unless I was free from my addiction and as a result of this newfound God-given freedom, I'm a new man walking with the Lord and the temptation of smoking crack really does not phase me that much. Don't get me wrong, I think about it from time to time and think about all that I have lost in the process of being a crackhead and I'm just thankful, so thankful to Jesus Christ for being here on the land of the living or the land of the dying depending how you view it; enabling me to write this book, hoping and praying that some man, woman, boy or girl will learn from these experiences of mine and everyone else in this book, that the road to drug addiction is nothing but pain and misery; a falsification of life through the eyes of Satan. But victory today is mine through Jesus Christ, The Son of The Living God.

At times when life gets hard and I can't seem to bare my burdens, I start to sing this particular song that gives me strength to carry on.

PRECIOUS LORD
Precious Lord, take my hand
Lead me on and let me stand
I am tired, I am weak, I am worn
Through the storm and through the night
Lead me on to the light
Take my hand precious Lord
And lead me on

One more thing I like to say is to the people who are still suffering from the addiction to crack or any other drug—try Jesus, you tried everything else; just give him a try. I know if God can change me, he can do it for you too but you've got to give him a serious try. Just pray and ask him to deliver and guide you from your addiction and he will. That's the thing about God; he never changes. He is there for you; just call him, and try him.

Only one thing has to come from you and that is this. YOU MUST HAVE A MADE-UP MIND. Don't kid yourself; have a made-up mind and be steadfast and unmovable in all that you do.

God Bless.

DENIAL

WHAT IS DENIAL? DENIAL IS WHEN someone who has a chemical substance abuse problem, be it alcohol or drugs, and will not look in the mirror and admit to themselves and say, "I have a problem." They give every other excuse except accepting the truth. "I'm not hooked." And the worst one of all is: "I can control it." Let me tell you firsthand it is all a lie and the first person that tells you they can control it must have seen God's face and that is how much control they have in actuality. Very few and only a very few people can and you ask them how personally when you visit them at the cemetery. I have not met one as of yet.

To be in denial is running from the truth and if you cannot face the truth, you cannot face yourself. Some people put off denial by playing the role that everything is okay. They refuse to see the reflection of self. Why would a person in a sick condition refuse to address such an important issue? Why indeed? There is only one reason and that reason is fear. Someone has said that fear is **F**alse **E**vidence **A**ppearing To Be **R**eal. Fear will make a person hide from him or herself. Fear brings out insecurity in the false form of security. Now, what does that mean? Simple, the insecurity that a person really feels and tries to harbor is camouflaged by things that are of the flesh such as money, cars, houses, land, jewelry, clothes, hiding behind things because things look good and things impress people and people being impressed by things cannot see that a person is really hiding from the truth.

Jesus said, "You shall know the truth and the truth shall set you free." The first thing that any addict or chemical dependent person needs to do is to face the truth and stop being in denial of that truth. Whether you are a functional addict or a professed addict, you still are an addict.

Once you face the truth and acknowledge the truth you will have conquered half the battle and the rest will come that much easier for you. Stop denying; rather stop lying to yourself. You can fool some of the people some of the time. You can fool some of the people all the time but you can't fool yourself or God none of the time.

HEALTH

IS STAYING ALIVE AND BEING HEALTHY a good enough reason for you to continue living? What a stupid, silly, ignorant question, right; wrong. This is true for so many addicts who are suffering day in and day out through the ever-elusive addiction to crack cocaine. It diminishes your health physically, mentally and spiritually so quickly that you don't even see it happening but others around you do. The continuous rapid loss of weight happens so fast that a strong turbulent wind can blow you over, facetiously speaking; but not that much.

The torment that you take your body through is relentless. Hooked on crack takes away your appetite (most people, very few can maintain their weight) and when they do eat, usually it's not the right foods that are nutritious for good health because smoking crack shrinks your stomach, killing your desire to eat even if you want to. In most instances, it's fast foods and sweets. Your mind is so cluttered and unclear that you don't and can't make positive and coherent decisions that will normally help you in life because of the poison that is absorbed into your mind. Why? You might ask; the answer is simple: you don't care.

Some people hooked on crack fail to do the simple things that normal everyday people do to their bodies, such as taking a shower or bathing, wearing the same clothes, not combing or bushing their hair or even their teeth for that matter; disgusting but oh so true. Now, don't be fooled, there are also a lot of crack addicts who do maintain their personal hygiene quite well and you would never know that they are a junkie addicted to crack cocaine. These people are functional addicts but believe this, they too are suffering with the delusion "I'm in control."

Let me tell you firsthand, no one, absolutely no one, can control Satan, the devil (except God) would you agree, of course; and that is what crack cocaine is. It's the spirit of Satan in its demonic spiritual form, taking control of your mind. In essence the person addicted to crack is mentally ill. I know it's hard to take like that but it is true.

GEARY

THE FIRST DRUG I EVER USED was alcohol in 1963. I was a young teenager then and I was curious. Drugs never really fascinated me but everyone else was indulging in them and it seemed to me the thing to do. My curiosity began to grow and I started using cocaine; crack, and from crack I used heroin which was my drug of choice because it made my sex life better. At least this was what I thought at the time. Altogether, I used drugs for about 23 years. I lost a lot during those years that I can never recover. I went to jail, then to prison, no place to be somebody; this was back in 1992. While in prison at San Quentin I gave myself to NA (Narcotics Anonymous) because that was the only thing I could do at the time to keep hope alive within my life as a convict locked up behind prison walls because of drugs. My use of them brought me to that stop sign and I had no other choice but to continue to live as an addict or go straight.

So, I attended those meetings, along with going to church, coming to the realization that I could not control the everlasting addiction of drugs, crack in particular. So, I surrendered. I turned it over to my Higher Power, God.

As a child I grew up in San Francisco in the Bayview Hunters Point District, one of many ghettos within the city, I was not a bad child nor was I a good child; I just got into a lot of trouble as kids do in the hood. I would go to school just to go and hang out with my friends. Although when I went to school, I never stayed; cutting classes was my major.

Since being released from prison in 1992, I have not and dare not take that road of misery and self-destruction again. If I do I might as well put a gun to my head and pull the trigger; that is how serious I am about the well-being of my life. Crack and no other drug have a space in my heart, mind, body and soul. It's been five years of being clean and sober; within those years I have accomplished quite a bit. I now own three businesses, a Bar-B-Que Restaurant, Rudy's; a beauty shop; and a beauty supply company. You might ask how; simple, I don't use anymore and my mind is clear, enabling me to make cohesive and right decisions.

My father came to me one day and said, "Son, if you don't stop using dope, when I die you will not get any of my inheritance."

I started laughing and said, "I'm your son."

He said, "It's not me, it's your mother and your sister, and when I die, they're going to get a shoebox and fill it with a lot of newspaper and put some money on top of it and by you being a fool you'll be satisfied with that."

But before he died I went to the penitentiary and got clean. He passed away.

I was clean and as a result of that I am now doing pretty good for myself and I often thank him for those words that helped me realize the true meaning of life and that I am not the fool that he thought I was. "Thanks, Dad."

Reminiscing on my life as a drug addict, I considered myself a cut above the rest. I would not just rob and steal. My hustle was real in the name of money; pimping whores and faggots, because in the game I was taught it did not matter where your money came from—a woman or a man—just as long as you got your money. Money at that time was my God and this was how I came up.

People find it hard to believe that an addict is an addict and the bad thing about being an addict is that you don't know you are an addict until it is too late. You fool yourself; you lie to yourself thinking that you are not but you are and this the calamity about being addicted: you don't even think you are an addict and by the time you realize it, it's a little bit too late to turn around until something stops you in your tracks.

You think you are strong, that your intelligence increases and your awareness becomes keen but in actuality you are weak and eventually you are going to die from using drugs. I remember seeing my brother die. I was living in a hotel and he had just hit the bricks, got out of penitentiary that is, and he came in with a sack of dope and I told him: "You not gonna be shooting that dope in my pad."

He went to the other room, him and a couple of his dope fiend buddies, and they started shooting that dope, heroin. I was in the other room with my wife, getting high snorting heroin and smoking weed. We were just chilling. After some time had elapsed, my wife said to me: "You better go and see what's going on." I walked into the room and my brother has been stripped butt naked by his homies; and they were trying to walk him around the room. He had overdosed. We were trying to bring him back around to life from the acute unconscious state that he was in.

Can you believe it; for ten hours we were doing things, trying to revive him. We even went to the extreme of shooting more dope into his veins, that was insane in and of itself but we did not know what to do. So, finally we took him to the hospital. Now, one might wonder why we did not rush him to the hospital as soon as this happened; the answer is simple: we were scared and afraid of what the consequences of the law might be as a result of our using illegal drugs.

When we finally made it to the hospital, he lived for two days in a coma and the doctor said his brain had died. This was my big brother, my only brother. You would think that after seeing all that it would do something to me and turn me around to make a change in my life but it didn't. I just got me some more dope and kept on going, that is what it meant to me.

Sometimes I have dreams, dreams about using again, a plate full of heroin and I'm getting loaded...then I wake up and realize it was just a dream and I am so happy because I know if I ever use again, I will lose everything that I worked for and I cannot afford to lose everything again, especially my life.

During my addiction, I had everything a man could ask for. I had a wife, five children and I even had a mistress but after it was said and done, I had nothing; even the dog left. Now, that's really cold when you lose your dog, a man's best friend next to God. When my wife left, she left me the broom to clean up. I said: "screw that," and went to get some more dope.

My message today for those addicts who are still shooting up and smoking crack is this: God loves you, I love you and I also know that getting help ain't easy. I've said it many a day. "I'm going to get me some detox, methadone." But I had a cold woman and each time I would attempt to get clean, she would say go and buy some more dope and I did. When you finally do decide to quit, you've got to cut your dope fiend friends loose; change your environment, because if you go to bed with dogs you are going to wake up with fleas and that's a fact. Still in all; you've got to try to get clean and if you relapse, try it again and again because one day if you keep sincerely trying, you will make it.

When crack first came on the scene, my set didn't call it crack. It was freebase, which was cocaine in its purest form not the dope that they now have out there on the streets because we cooked the dope up ourselves and it was really good at that time. I recall when about ten of my buddies would get together on a Friday and Saturday, spend about $500 each; we did this with ease. Five hundred dollars wasn't nothing to us because we were players, pimps, hustlers, dope pushers, thieves and robbers; driving Cadillacs, Continentals, Limos, Vets, Benzes and the double Rs (Rolls Royce). We were more than living large; *we were large.* We had the finest clothes, expensive clothes and so much jewelry Mr. T, from *The A-Team*, didn't have nothing on us. Diamond rings on every finger, not just diamonds but carats. During that time it was no problem getting money, hustling; because my set respected the game. These days the youngsters don't respect the game and the game is all screwed up.

My crack addiction was so baffling, I couldn't figure it out. I remember once when I was on a two-week crack run, meaning I smoked crack every day and every night for two weeks straight. God, it's a wonder I am still alive today to share this with you because all I was doing was endangering my life for a traumatic heart attack but that is what happened. I only ate because I had to stay alive just to give my body some nourishment and I only slept when I could no longer keep my eyes open. Man, that was sick but then again I was sick; a diseased drug addict.

I got a job with the longshoremen and that work was very hard at times. So, therefore I couldn't get high until the weekend. I remember one weekend my wife put me out for doing something stupid. I don't remember what it was but I went to my mistress' and stayed there for the weekend. She went out and bought some crack and we started getting high. All of a sudden, I heard someone whistling upstairs in the house and I'm tripping, I thought that she had another man upstairs in the room.

I said, "Bitch, you have somebody upstairs."

She said, "No, you just tripping."

My partner was there with me getting high and we both heard the whistling or thought we heard it. So, we called the police; now that is how hard we were tripping. They came and saw that we were high and told us to "Get on," and left.

That same night we went out to buy some more crack and ran into the same cops. They just laughed and said, "Yeah, you guys high on the crack." We paid them no attention and went back to the house to continue to get high. Here I am smoking and smoking and I hear the whistling again. I grabbed my woman along with a butcher knife and took her upstairs and I was looking for this man who was in the house. I pulled her into the bedroom; put the dresser against the door and commenced choking her. Man, I was trying to kill her. She broke loose; her son jumped out the window searching for someone to help his mother but I ended up leaving her house to go and get some more dope. I damn near killed her all because I was tweaking, tripping off of crack. Ain't that something?

Now, I never really liked crack but I did it because my woman liked it and I was not about to let her smoke up all my money. So, I might as well smoke with her. I even started smoking cigarettes and that's the last thing in life I thought I would ever do but I did. Ain't that weird? But when you are using dope ain't nothing weird. That damn crack made me feel like a fool because I could not go back outside after smoking it until I came down because of the paranoia and its overwhelming effect; the sensation of how it made me feel. Ultimately, I lost a lot of money waiting to come down and by the time I did get back out on the streets, all the money that I was supposed to have made was gone.

Today, I don't need any of it; a drink of alcohol, crack or heroin, and when I have that feeling come on me to pick and use I just pray and the Lord delivers me from it, every time and I thank him for it. Now, I still like my money, yes I do and I stopped liking drugs and if it was not for God, my Higher Power, I'd be out there right now, sucking the glass peter, the pipe.

I still have friends who are using. I don't have anything to do with them but if they ever need me, I'll be there just as fast as I can because I know it's a sickness and in a lot of cases they just cannot help themselves. Sometimes when I would run out of drugs and lay down in my bed, I would think of ways to get some crack and heroin; remember I was a longshoreman at this time and it was no problem for me to steal merchandise off the ship to sell and or trade for dope, none at all. I had the security guard in my pocket because he was a dope fiend too. I became a thief and there were other people working on the docks with me sharing the same sickness that I had, as a junkie, first class, and they were thieves too.

We would get together on the weekends; get paid after

working all week and smoke it all up; spending our entire check on crack and we were making a thousand dollars or more per week; take home pay, with no problems, tax exempt. We would not file taxes at the end of the year because we were too cool for that.

Anyway, after spending all our money, every cent of a thousand dollars on dope the Friday night when we got paid, me and a few more waterfront people—my partners in crime— would seek out ships that had good cargo on them; merchandise worth money. It did not matter what it was just as long as it brought money. Stuff like Levi's, stereos, meat, shrimp, lobster, steak and clothes and sometimes we got real lucky even more than what we could have dreamed of; especially if we found a ship that had the real expensive clothes, like ladies and men's suites, leather and fur coats. Expensive stuff that brought monetary value we would steal and sell.

We would make what we spent the night before in a matter of a few hours, hands down, no problem. It got so good and so easy that we mistreated our hustle and got greedy and that is the one rule you are always supposed to follow: "Don't get greedy." The man started watching his merchandise; so much so that we had to back off and by this time my addiction was so overpowering I started doing things I thought I would never do in life.

At night I would drive around looking for something steal, find cars, mostly Volkswagens because they came equipped with good stereos, and I would steal them, trade them for dope. Ain't that insane? Here I was making a thousand dollars a week and out in the world breaking in cars, stealing stereos, just like a common thief but that is the thing about being a drug addict, a user; you start to do things beyond the comprehension of your normality.

My addiction got so bad that I would not even go to work and if I did go, I went to steal. You see, being on the waterfront you had a choice to work or not work and if I elected to go to work on a job and there was nothing worth stealing, I would leave and go try to make some money so I could get high. That was an option you had as a longshoreman; if you did not like the job that was assigned to you, you could leave, go home and come back the next day and go out on another job on another day.

Well, things got so bad that I would have my woman go out and steal so that I could support my drug habit; it wasn't no thing. We would pack up the kids in the car and go shopping, stealing; because keeping my high on was my priority. Sometimes I would find another thief who stole meat. We called them "Cattle rustlers." Out to get some beef, mostly steaks but limited to any other kind of meat, as long as we could sell it. It was all about getting some money by any means necessary to support my crack addiction.

Now this is radically insane when a person will not even go to work to make money because he wants to get high smoking crack but now that I am clean and I have my businesses flowing, everything is all good. I even have my jewelry back. When I was deep in my addiction, I would sell all my gold, diamonds, watches, rings, necklaces, bracelets. I had so much jewelry… I reflect now and say, "Ain't that a blimp." I traded all that stuff in the name of crack, the rock, a dirty shame.

The pawn shop man was glad to see me coming; he even knew me by name. He would say, "Hey, Geary" because he knew I had some real good jewelry and that when I came to his shop and sold my gems I was not coming back to get them. You know what, sometimes when things got a little tight, I would go to that same pawn shop and pawn a piece or two but always returned and picked them up because I'm not stuck on stupid, stuck on crack, no not anymore. Now, when he sees me driving up in my El Dorado all he can say is: "There goes, Geary, he's doing." And I am and it is all because of the Lord and his goodness.

Now, I got so much material stuff I could sell it hands down but I'm not. I ain't going to sell nothing because I worked too hard for my stuff to just throw it away; worked too hard in my life to just smoke it up, worked too hard in my life to lay it all down in the name of crack; no, not me. No, maybe before but not now. The only thing I'm selling is barbeque and I've got the best in town just like I had the best dope, now I've got the best sauce.

I'd like to say to all the suffering addicts out there today: I love you. God loves you. If no one hugs you today, come by my shop, I will hug you, because I love you. But the whole thing is that you got to try. No one, absolutely no one can succeed if they don't try. Just take it one day at a time. I still take it one day at a time and it's been five years and I'm still taking it that way, one day at a time. I don't do a lot of studying. I do go to church to thank God for his goodness in saving me. Every first Sunday I do my best to be in his service and take my sacrament and it's just a thing about taking the Lord's Supper, his blood and his body that revives me and keeps me going on and on and all that I am saying to you is that if you don't try to stay clean, you will never get clean.

Man, it was hard for me, a lot of miserable nights and days in my life. Life is still not that good sometimes but that's how life is but only this time I can deal with it today on today's terms but if I was loaded, man, there is no telling where I might be right now; dead or in prison who knows where, there's just no telling.

So for the addict who is still out there, strung out, just try it, try it, and then try it again. One day you will succeed if you truly try it with all your heart, mind and soul. I know it's not easy and you cannot do it overnight. It took a long time for me to give it up but I did and if I can, so can you. Just take it one day at a time and after you give it one day, give it another day, then another day and pretty soon you will be surprised and before you know it, you too will be clean. Go to meetings—Narcotics Anonymous, Alcohol Anonymous; go to church, try church and pray, give it to God or your Higher Power—whatever it takes. Get on your knees and just surrender and ask God to take it away from you and he will.

Hey, nothing comes overnight and when you ask God to deliver you and you don't get delivered immediately, do not worry because your mind is matching your heart and more than that, you cannot doubt what he can do for you. Believe you me, nothing is going to come to you that you ask for in the next twilight hour. You go to work on it and stay with it and it will come but you have to have faith.

Now, I get everything I ask for, everything; all because I'm clean. When things get bad for me, I get on my knees and pray and things start to happen for me. It may not happen when I want it to but it happens. So, be strong, try to surrender and take it one day at a time.

PARANOIA

CRACK COCAINE WILL MAKE YOU SO paranoid (at least 90% of people using it) that when smoking it after a period of time, you just start to trip. Some people call it tweaking, you start hearing everything out of the ordinary: people knocking at your door, police waiting to break in, such things like that and this is just the surface but it goes further than that. It's really extraordinary and very frightening or even comical if you are not a user to see someone walking around with a knife or even a gun in their hand while under its influence waiting to attack anything that moves, looking under the bed, behind closed and opened doors, even running away from your own home, thinking someone is there. Many users who are getting high have gotten hurt, some seriously by someone else who is tripping out from smoking crack. I remember an instance where we were exchanging crack war stories when this one guy shot through his front door because he thought someone was trying to break in and it was the paperboy coming to collect for the paper.

Another time a friend was driving home after smoking crack and thought he was being followed, so he pulled the police over and asked the officer to follow him home a few blocks away. Another time this guy was running from people whom he thought were chasing him. He ended up on a roof and the fire department was called to help get him off. He was scared that the demons were after him. (Well, they were.)

All of these stories are true and there are many more as you will see when you read through this book. Now, you would think that a person going through all of this drama might not want to freak themselves out in this fashion but they do it again and again and again. Legally speaking, they are insane. I kid you not; at that time and moment sanity is out the door. There is no control over your imagination and the evil thoughts, sinful desires that become manifested while smoking crack cocaine. Some addicts are okay with this behavior because they are in essence an instrument being used and played by the prince of darkness, Satan.

FAMILY

CRACK COCAINE, ALSO KNOWN ON THE streets as the rock, yale, ice cream, vanilla and work. The last term really gets me to thinking "work"; yes, working on destroying yourself because that is exactly what it does. Crack destroys your family almost instantaneously; right before your eyes. It separates the husband from the wife and vice versa. It alienates you from your parents, children, sisters and brothers, and all the rest of your family. Domestic duties around your home become passé. It makes you lazy, not wanting to go to work; some people even become homeless recipients of the state welfare system enabling them to use to live and live to use and even worse, smoking crack disassociates the user from the life and love of the family that they once knew and that is an absolute truth.

It is really devastating to see within a person's home the effects of the addiction to crack and its consequences of damnation. This does not happen to everyone who is addicted but no matter what the difference or how the percentages are, it's still a no-win situation. Some people lose their family in midst of addiction; this is not limited to gender. Crack has no partiality, black, white, red, yellow or brown; it does not discriminate just like God and Satan. It has no respect of person. Some people lose their homes, cars and any other monetary or material values that they have accumulated and possessed over the years of hard work. Swish; down the drain in the bottomless pit sucking you dry.

Many people using crack will fail to pay their bills and if they do they are usually robbing Peter to pay Paul. Some disregard their children's well-being, keeping unkempt homes and many a day have little or no food for the family to eat except on the days when mom or dad gets paid. This is so catastrophic and incomprehensible, yet it is real.

You know the sadness of this is the neglect, love, time and attention that the children should be receiving and that is the reason why some of the young people are the people that they are. They do not have enough prime adult examples to lead them in the right direction. To not care whether your children eat or do not eat or even that their clothes are clean and that they themselves are groomed properly is pathetic but oh so true. Don't misunderstand what I am saying to you; these people who are addicted and under the control of the submissional influence of this drug called crack, along with the substance of alcohol, are sick with this chemical poisoning disease, do love their children but due to their addiction they fail to show it by giving their children the attention they rightfully deserve all because of their addictions; not all addicts fit into this realm but most do.

This lifestyle causes drastic ramifications. Some children rebel by not doing well in school and even dropping out. Some become resentful and very hard; failing to respect themselves, mother and father or any other authoritative figure of society. On the other hand, there are those young people who have seen what drug addiction can do a person and they stay away from drugs and alcohol altogether. However, on the other side, it's hard for many young people to cope with normal living when they see their mother and or father strung out on crack; some in prison, drug addicts, alcoholics and some even dead from living the street life and you wonder why they seek out gangs or other peers for refuge. Many times this is the reason but in actuality all they need is more love, time and attention from mom and dad. Some are living in single-family homes, which makes it even more trying for that one person to raise a family but this is the way it is.

The question is: how much does your family mean to you? These days it takes a lot to make a family be as one; especially since there are so many single mothers trying to carry the load as both mother and father. Even if you do have a member of your family who is strung out on crack and I know that this may be hard for some family members to read and take it to heart but you must continue to love them and help them. Don't get me wrong; do not enable them to stay in the position that they are in. Sometimes you have to love them from a distance. Do not help to support their habit but rather try to reach them through speaking, through prayer, through counseling and whatever other means you can use to help save your son or daughter, mother or father, husband or wife, etc. It is your duty. It is especially your duty if they are sincerely trying to walk the straight and narrow.

I know that it is not easy to forgive and forget but you have to remember above all the treachery that is your blood and if you can by any means help save your own blood then that is what you do. Do it, do not let hate prevail over your love. Who knows you might be the key, the missing link to help them live a normal life again.

JOHN

HELLO, MY NAME IS JOHN AND I am a recovering crack addict but, thanks to the grace of God, it has now been five years and six months since I have picked up the pipe and smoked crack cocaine. Let me start by telling you a little bit about myself; how it was, how it all happened (my addiction) and how it is now, today. In the beginning I was a young child brought up in this big world together with my mother and father. They both were very loving and caring parents, hard-working responsible people bringing up their children. Our family consisted of five children. I was in the middle of two brothers and two younger sisters and was also the elected one of the children to go beyond the call of duty. The one who was put up front to make things happen, the one who was most likely to succeed.

Now that I think about it, I was always being pushed to do better than the rest of my siblings; always put on the middle limb to be the one example of perfection or to handle all of the grunt work. If there was anything new to be tried and completed, I was the one who handled the task. The entire family including my brothers and sisters pushed me, I was the sacrificial lamb.

We had big wedding celebration one night when I was five years old for my grandmother. At that time all of my uncles, aunts and a host of relatives were in attendance for this gala affair and they gave me some champagne, all that I could drink. I remember going around to each and every member of the family asking them for a sip of their champagne. Before too long my head was spinning in a whirlpool from drinking the bubbly stuff. I loved the bubbles, the effervescent sound of them popping continuously in the glass was like magic. Now you see them, now you don't; it was great. I got drunk at the age of five and it was a beautiful feeling, great. Maybe that was the start of my addiction. As a matter of fact, it was. I could never forget the experience because that was the first time the *Apollo* spaceship went up in outer space.

I did not drink after that until the age of thirteen, which was in itself much too young but due to the peer pressure of my friends who were indulging in drinking alcohol and me trying to fit in, I did succumb and yielded not myself to the enslavement thus becoming a part and an acceptance into the bondage of addiction.

During this time I had job working with my dad in his janitorial business; something that I had always done since the age of five. I had to work. I was never able to say: "No, I don't want to go to work." Even though I would have rather stayed at home and studied, which I did sometimes prefer to do. However, still in all, I knew that it was a necessity for me to render my services to the livelihood of our family's survival. It just was not possible for me to study on many occasions because our parents were not able to make ends meet on the income they had coming in. We could not survive unless I contributed along with my other brothers helping my father. All of us had to work. Later, he turned the business over to his brother, my uncle, and we had to continue working for my uncle; rather we were forced to work for him.

The crowd of people I hung out with drank alcohol, smoked weed and cigarettes, my older brother included. I would more

56

often than not feel left out because he and his friends never included me in their activities of partying. I remember watching my brother get high and saying to myself: "I'm going tell Mother." He's smoking weed but I never did. Then, one night as fate would have it; we went to this party at the beach and one of his friends asked me if I wanted to hit it, the joint that is and I said, "Yeah." And after I hit it, I couldn't quit it. It was on, that was the ultimate thing for me. At this time in my life I did not know that the ultimate would not always be the ultimate as I knew it at that time because this was the birth of my addiction. My world had finally come together at least so it seemed.

Feeling like I was now a part of the circle; being accepted, a perfect fit sitting on top of the world, everything had finally come together. I felt like I was a success in life achieving the ultimate goal; fulfilling the emptiness of the void that was missing within my life not knowing or realizing at this time that I was just heading for trouble. Even though I thought the void was filled, I did not know it was truly vacant, an evaporation; temporarily leaving me as quick as I could inhale and exhale the smoke that was polluting my lungs. So, therefore, I had to keep on filling it again and again and eventually graduating to higher substances to get high on.

At the age of sixteen I started drinking alcoholic beverages of all sorts; gin, brandy, vodka, bourbon, scotch, tequila, wine and beer. It did not matter as long as it was alcohol. I smoked weed every day on a regular basis; not just one or two joints. Marijuana became my God and I worshipped the herbal plant of green. I had to have it and so I did. Two years passed, I am eighteen now and I graduated again not from high school, mind you, but to even more drug use pills and cocaine.

I began dropping pills, snorting and smoking cocaine mixed with weed; putting it in joints, cigarettes and any other way we could use it, staying high all the time. Later on I was introduced to freebase, which is the purest form of cocaine to get high on by putting the powder in a cooker bottle mixed with a little baking soda thus eliminating all the impurities from the cocaine powder and smoking it in a pipe. This was cool for a while but someone later on invented crack, the most deadliest and demonic form of cocaine that I ever indulged in my life.

I would freebase so much coke; getting so loaded that I wanted to turn all my friends on to this wonderful new experience of getting high because this stuff was real good. After a while I became dependent on it and I had to have more and more and more; especially when smoking crack, it took the place of smoking freebase cocaine.

All the money I worked for from my job was spent on crack cocaine in one night after getting paid. When I ran out of dope and all my money was spent, I would go out and hustle; stealing, so that I could have money not only for some crack but for the survival of supporting my addiction to get high for the rest of the day or the week; whatever it would take, I had to have money.

This experience made me part of the scum of the world; me and my friends who were also addicts. You know the old adage "Birds of a feather flock together." We would go out on "Missions" as we would call them; meaning any illegal activity to get some money in order to get high. We would take the 22 Filmore Bus and pick pockets; take peoples wallets, purses and anything else that they had of value. The reason we rode this particular bus route was because it was about 10 miles long, or so it seemed, was always crowded with people and this enabled us to do our crime without attracting too much attention.

I even stole from my parents; money and anything else that was in the house that was worth money to help support my addiction to crack. I don't feel proud about it but once again I had to have money in order to get high and I would do this by any means necessary.

My parents got tired of me stealing from them and living the life of a drug addict in their home. So, one day, they kicked me out of their house. I ended up living in the Tenderloin, downtown, south of Market Street, better known as the Lion's Den, or The Razor, because if you did not know how to survive in its environment of murderers, rapists, robbers, drug addicts, alcoholics, pimps, whores, thieves, transvestites, homosexuals, sadomasochists, and any other lower than life perpetrators, you would get eaten alive or cut to shreds. It was known as the concrete jungle of the two-legged scums of the earth who had only one thing in mind and that was to steal your soul. This was the skid road of the "Everybody Loves" great tourist city of San Francisco, the city that sits on top of the hill, where you can reach for the stars riding on the cable care, hypothetically speaking, yet, literally. You can get killed in a heartbeat living in The Razor and this is still a reality today. Yet, here I was living in The Tenderloin.

It was a terrible experience for me; one that I would not wish upon any of my foulest of enemies. What made it so bad for me is that I was not a hard-core street person or a criminal (ex-convict). So I became one of the few people who lived there who was preyed upon by the lions (people predators living off the weak vessels within its habitat). They would devour you if given the chance with fangs of blood dripping from their mouths, with the fangs of blood penetrating from their eyes of death. They had cold eyes that looked right through you, eyes of anger and rage, eyes of malice and deceit, eyes that would stalk you with their fangs of blood waiting to steal your soul, waiting for the right moment to attack you and kill you whether it be necessary or not, depending on their state of mind. This was the Lion's Den and where I did live for a period of time and made it through only because God was with me.

Shortly after living in the Tenderloin and getting burned by the lowlifes who dwelled there. I mean it was so degrading and humiliating; yet I could not figure out how to leave the environment that I was living in. Now, I know firsthand how a person can get caught up in the web of addiction, in the web of darkness and sin and not make it back; a web of sorrow and sadness, depression and oppression compressed deep down in your soul and all you have to do is stay on its track; riding the rails pressing straightforward and full speed ahead heading for hell. One thing is for certain: if you stay on this track, you won't finish the race because in reality it's not a race. It is a trap; a set-up designed to steal your soul.

I remember giving the one dude fifty dollars to go and buy some crack. He never came back. Now, I look at that past experience and laugh because I was fool but that was the makeup of my character as a person. I have never been a cruel or cold person but the people mixed up in the drug world are just that mean and cruel and if they don't start out that way, they end up that way. It's inevitable. Sometimes you can't tell the difference because you don't know whom to trust and even if you do; the closet one you can trust will end up burning you somewhere along the line. There is no trust amongst addicts; there is only betrayal of trust. There are only those who are walking in the counsel of the ungodly. There are only those who sit at the table and break bread with you and will give you up and sell you out for less than thirty pieces of silver. In the drug world someone is always standing there waiting to stab you in the back. One night I was getting high and ended up in the hospital at the San Francisco Psyche Ward. I think someone laid a Mickey on me (put something in my drink) and my mind was messed up. Things go so bad for me that I would end up in the psyche ward or in jail every month for about three years; this is how bad my personal addiction was controlling me. It was getting to be very sickening.

I was living on the streets, pushing a shopping cart that became my personal dresser drawer that carried my life; picking up aluminum cans, bottles, plastic or anything that was recyclable; whatever I could get in order to get high. It came to a point where getting high was not fun for me anymore, getting high was not all that I thought it was. Getting high had caused me misery. Getting high had caused me so much grief and devastation. Getting high was a nightmare. I was broken to the lowest degree, yet I could not stop getting high. I could not stop smoking crack. I kept on getting high. Getting high had become a curse that I could not break free from until one night, as a homeless person living on the streets of San Francisco, a night I will never forget.

Yes, it got so bad for me that I became one of the many

people whose home became the streets all because of my addiction to drugs; all behind the trickery of crack. I had burned all of my bridges, no one trusted me and even wanted me around them. That's another thing about being a drug addict. Whether it was crack or heroin, crank, alcohol or whatever, no one trusts you because you screwed over the people who loved you. You messed up one time too many and now there is no hope of reconciliation with those people unless you become clean and even then it still will take some time.

Well, this one particular night I got arrested. Now that I am clean, I call it "Rescued." I was riding on the BART Train. (Bay Area Rapid Transit) and I snuck into the station, got on a train and started riding, trying to find a nice comfortable seat so that I could get some sleep without being in the elements of the outdoors. The train stopped and the operator came, found me asleep and told me to get off. He was talking to me in a very disrespectful manner. Then again, looking at my appearance at that time, I too would have considered myself a bum. I was dirty and stinking. I had not taken a bath in a long time. So, I guess, in essence I was a hobo riding the train. He called the BART police. They came to escort me off the train. In the process it became physical and I was charged with resisting arrest, assault on police officer who said that I had broken one of his fingers and was taken to jail.

While I was in jail, I began to think about my life without any excuses, without being in denial, without blaming anyone else except the one who deserves to take the blame, which was me. I began to make an assessment of myself, a truth that only I could do and in doing so I found that there was no other way for me in life except the road that leads to Christ.

I gave my life to Jesus. You've got to understand; I was either going to the penitentiary or the graveyard. So, I made a commitment; not a verbal commitment but rather spirit-filled heart and soul commitment to surrender my life to Christ and today I am a clean and sober man. Thanks to Jesus Christ, I have been delivered. Today, I have a job. I am married; a newlywed, two years now, with a brand-new baby girl just born a week ago. March 1996. God has delivered me from the addiction of crack cocaine and alcohol and I thank him for saving my life.

All of that time I thought I was fulfilling the void in my life getting high, searching for the answer of life; thought that smoking crack was a recreational thing to do; it never was. Now I know the void could have never been filled had it not been for Jesus Christ dying for a sinner like me and yet still loving me. I would just like to say to all of the people—men, women, boys and girls—that if you are still strung out suffering from the addiction of crack or any other drug or false chemical substance trying to fill the void, I ask you today as you read this story along with the rest within these pages to try God. He did it for me. And I know if God can save me, he can save you too.

There's a scripture in The Holy Bible that says, "A just man may fall seven times, he rises again but the wicked will fall into mischief" (Proverb 24:16). (He) God picked me up again and again; giving me a chance to live for him.

I just want to let you know one more thing. You do not have to be addicted to crack or any other chemical substance to try Jesus, but if you are, why not let him in today and see what a difference your life can be with him at the helm.

Thank you.

DEALERS

YOU WHO ARE HOOKED; LET'S GET one thing straight and clear right now. The people selling this poisonous drug called crack do not care about you in the least degree. I have seen it and experienced it over and over, oh so many times. You spend one, two or three hundred dollars, maybe more, with a dealer in a period of a week or two; sometimes maybe that much per day if you have it and, mind you, this is on a small scale in comparison to the drug money that's out in the streets and you go back to that same dealer with no money and you cannot even get or barely get ten dollars on credit.

To them you're a crackhead, tweaker, thief, junkie; the scum of the earth and they are the parasites waiting to eat you alive all in the name of crack but as long as you keep spending your money with them then you are their best friend all day long; stop and to them you're worthless.

They give you lines like: "I just sold my last rock." "I don't have anymore." "Check with me in about an hour," or words to that effect and many other tales to keep you at bay but then again they paid for their product (drugs) and have been in a lot of cases burnt by the promises of being paid back.

In essence to a dealer you don't deserve any respect; you're a whore and crack is your pimp and the cold part about it is you pay to get screwed. Excuse me, you pay to get f-----. (I thought it was supposed to be the other way around.) So do not be disillusioned; any person, rather any fool, who would spend all his money on crack just to get high deserves exactly what they get, rather what they don't get which is nothing because they have no more money.

So do not be misguided by the smiles and the hellos, especially with closet dealers; the ones who have good jobs, family, nice house and the amenities of a good person. Those who portray the roles of everyday people but are drug dealers in the closet. These people are hard to pick out of the crowd because they don't give themselves away to be drug dealers but they too mean you absolutely no damn good. I have seen them all; dealers on streets and dealers in the home. They will talk about crackheads in a demeaning manner. Some even go so far as to spit on them, kick them, beat them up and laugh at them. They call them stupid for being stuck on stupid; take away your money and to them you're nothing but a crackhead. Bottom line.

LATE BLOOMERS

THIS IS A GROUP OF INDIVIDUALS I FEEL the deepest contempt from the bottom of my heart and that's no lie. Let me first define exactly what a late bloomer is. It's a person whose over the age of 25—I believe by this time in your life maturity should have set in and enough experiences of life to let you know what is good and what is bad. However, there are some who will tempt the hand of fate thinking that they are above normality, that they can indulge and conquer trying crack cocaine for a first time and enjoy it. Thus befitting, hooked; a junkie strung out on crack.

The reason for my feelings and beliefs are so tumultuous that I find it constrained to believe that someone who has life in so much perspective would dare defile and take the chance of addiction and start smoking crack. I must tell you, it is band enough to start smoking crack at an early age. Come to think of it, most people strung out on drugs do no start out on hard drugs they gradually increase their use of drugs because they have become immune to what they are using and need a higher high to get high. But it is even worse if you start at the age of 25 or older.

65

Be it said right now: if you do, you are in for the most terrifying ride of your life that no roller coaster you ever rode can compare and that is a fact.

Let me be upfront totally. If you start this fantasy/reality check at these ages of your life, in all honesty you may not make it back. Back to what? Your family, friends and loved ones and, most importantly, back to yourself and your normal being. You might even lose your mind. You might have a heart attack the first time you take a hit and die and if not do remember this: it takes a lot of time to get clean and sober from this particular drug and any other for that matter; time which life may or may not permit you to have. Is the risk worth the injury?

Is it worth the game to lose everything you have worked so diligently for? You will end up in one of three situations as so many others have already. (1) Losing everything: family, friends, and all your material values you have accumulated over the years. (2) Homeless (3) Prison or (4) Death.

And if none of the above, one thing is dead sure; misery will be your friend, especially in your spirit.

Make no doubt about it; if you get hooked at this stage of your life, you will be giving your soul to Satan. In essence that is exactly what you will be doing, is it worth it? Only you can answer that question.

WANDA

HELLO, MY NAME IS WANDA. I am a recovering alcoholic and crack addict. My parents migrated from Puerto Rico to San Francisco, California, to live where I was raised as a child. There were six children in our family; four girls and two boys. Daddy was a musician and he went on the road a lot and was hardly ever at home. During the times he was out of town my mother would go out with his friends. He had many friends and one at a time they became my mother's boyfriends; her lovers.

There were many parties at our house whenever Dad came home and a lot of drinking. Oh! A lot of drinking. I can recall as a small child, I was about four years old, my mother asked my godmother to baby-sit my siblings and me while she and my father went out partying and she did.

That night for some strange reason I couldn't sleep. Maybe it was the forces of darkness that kept me awake because what happened next should not have happened to a young girl like me at my tender age but it did. My godmother was cleaning the kitchen. I got up from my bed, asking her when my parents were coming back home. She said, "In a little while; go back to bed."

As I was lying there trying to go to sleep, there was a knock at the door. It was one of my mother's boyfriends. I could hear my godmother telling him that my father was back in town and that she was out with him partying at a nightclub. He said, "Okay, I'll call her later." I heard the door slam while she was still in the kitchen, singing as she cleaned. Later, she came in our room and said she was leaving. I asked her to leave the kitchen light on as she left.

Then all of sudden the stillness within the house broke and I heard something and realized there was someone in our house. It was the boyfriend. He had only pretended to leave and was hiding in my mother's closet. He came into my room where be began to molest me, and as this despicable deed was going on my mother and father came back home.

My mother walked into the room and started screaming and hollering while hitting him with a flurry of wild punches. I could hear my father's heavy footstep rushing down the hall at a fast pace asking, "What's going on?" In a fit of anger and hysteria, she told him and a real knockdown, drag-out fight broke out between the boyfriend and my father, who ended up kicking the guy out of the house. Strange, but after that night, we never spoke about what had happened to me on that dreadful occasion when I was raped.

The episode of that night changed me within as a child, as it would do any child. I would seldom play outside with the other children, rather electing to constantly stay inside near my mother. We became real close.

As time went on my sister and I started drinking. We were about ten years old at the time and we did not just drink beer or wine but hard alcohol as well. I figured it couldn't be that bad, especially since my mother was the one doing the pouring and Mom wouldn't do anything to hurt me, not her child. Right?

I can recall my mother showing me off to her and my father's friends as if I were her trophy; I hated it with a passion. I became a straight "A" student while in junior high school. My parents were very proud of me for this accomplishment. Although they felt this way, it was hard for me to understand and comprehend when they did not even show up for my graduation. Can you imagine that? It hurt so bad, it still affects me; sometimes in the worst way. This is when and where my addiction to chemical substance began; right after graduation from junior high school.

I started dropping pills, all kinds of pills, and drinking alcohol. It seemed to be a release of all the stress and the pressures of everyday life, which were so imperious and unyielding. It was so hard that I attempted to commit suicide at the age of fifteen. I took a lot of pills and heard my mother's voice in the back of my mind while in a fog saying, "Those kinds of pills won't kill a person." I failed and I'm glad I did; to this day, I'm glad.

Later, we moved from our place in the Mission District to Protrero Hill in the projects, the ghetto. About a year later I got a job working at the Old Mint on Fifth and Market Street where they used to make money. I used to see so much money that it was unbelievable. At that time I wasn't drinking or smoking because I was into my job whole-heartedly. Six months later I started drinking again. I was nineteen almost twenty.

I lost my true virginity to a younger guy, he was fifteen. It makes me laugh now when I think about that first time when I surrendered myself and had sexual intercourse but then at that time I wasn't thinking about how young he was because I was pretty young and inexperienced.

Working every day and making my own money put me on top of the world. My girlfriend, who was also my neighbor, became my very close friend. We would drink and pop pills together, having fun getting high. Then one day as I was preparing myself to go to go to work, she came by and asked me if I could help her get some pills, which I did. We hung out together for a few minutes and I told her that I had to go to work. She asked me to knock on her door before I left. While I was knocking at her door I saw my bus coming…I could hear my friend faintly in the distance saying, "Wait a minute, Wanda." The sound of her voice led me to believe that she was upstairs in her house but I had to go because I did not want to be late for work.

Two hours later, while I was at work, I received a telephone call from my mother bearing to me the tragic news as the Grime Reaper; my girlfriend had committed suicide. Numbness immediately fell within my spirit; darkness overshadowed my mind, with a heavy-laden heart of pain; burden down too hard to bear, a feeling of emptiness had come over my whole being. It took possession of my soul; the blackness of death. I knew from the moment of that experience that when the Angel of Death takes someone whom you love and care about, a part of you dies also.

Apparently, she had taken a gun and shot herself straight through the head. I remember asking my mother: "What happened?" She tried to console me as a mother's love for her child would do, but to no avail. Absorbed with dissipation and filled with disillusionment, hurt and pain; I broke down as tears began to fill my eyes, dropping heavily to the floor where I stood, drop after drop, suspended in the animation of time. I asked myself: "Am I here? Am I there? Where am I? Is this really real? Is this what life is supposed to be? Is this the end?" I don't know, I can't see. Although my eyes are open, I am blind, trapped in a world of despair. "This can't be, this can't be, this can't be." I kept saying to myself: "This can't be. It's not real." Denial of the truth self-evident, escapism is all I wanted; to get away, not to face the fact, but rather to slip, slide and dig my way to another place, to another space in time.

My supervisor tried to comfort me, told me to take a breather and I did. I popped another pill to ease the hurt and pain. I went home and crashed; that was all I could do at the time—get high, because I was sick and miserable, not knowing that the black hole of no return, death, was just becoming an acquaintance in my life and would spellbound me with its calamitous wretchedness for many a day.

My new boyfriend started trying to abuse me but I refused to let a young punk batter and try to hurt me. I retaliated by beating him with an extension cord. Soon, thereafter, I dissolved my relationship with him and hooked up with my brother's friend,

Miles. At this time I had two children, a daughter and a son, and Miles, my new man, who had just come into my life. He treated me real good and made feel very loved, just like a lady should be treated. He also introduced me to cocaine, something a real lady can do without. Oh What A Man!! It was the beginning of my end; the beginning of a painful and miserable life of addiction; the beginning of becoming one of Satan's servants; the beginning of a dying soul; a sheep being led to the slaughter of the blood alleys of the cement jungle captured in the demonic pit with Satan locked in a human body of flesh, not knowing or having a clue as to where I was going or whom I was going with. Only much later would I find out that I was riding as a passenger in a vehicle driven by the enemy of darkness on my way to hell while living yet in hell.

Miles and I started snorting cocaine, smoking weed and drinking alcohol. I didn't think I was an alcoholic or an addict at that time but I was. It's strange that some people who are alcoholics and or addicts don't think that they are.

We moved to an apartment down on Army Street, which was not too far from the projects five miles away. I would frequently go and visit my mother up on the hill, who, by this time, had divorced my father, and drank up all the liquor in her house. She would get angry when I did this and she would make me leave my children, kicking me out of her house because I would be intoxicated. When she did this, I would go home and start fighting Miles but he never would hit me back, at least not at this time but that would change. He was a good man. Things would eventually change, slowly but surely things would change, they always do when you become an addict. Isn't it strange how many men we women let abuse us and yet we still consider them good?

I became pregnant with my other daughter, Velva. Now, I had three kids: Felecia, Carl, and Velva. My life was wonderful, so I thought. I really had it going on but at the same time my man was taking my AFDC (welfare) check, and buying and selling dope; cocaine. Soon, after Velva's birth I became pregnant again with my second boy, Bradley Joe, and my drug use was really, really

71

heavy; snorting cocaine, smoking week and drinking alcohol.

Well, it was time for my baby to come. Miles accompanied me to the hospital. He came into the hospital with me and witnessed the gift of our son being born in the world. It was a very joyful and special occasion for both of us. He left and did not even come back the next day; just dropped me off like a sack of potatoes. Man, that was cold. I knew he was partying and celebrating the birth of his son but I was alone in the hospital and pissed off. Still, I had a feeling of consolation within my soul and that is what the use of drugs can do to a person after so many days, weeks, months and years of addiction. It steals your soul with the falsity that what you are doing is okay. The consummation of this feeling prevailed nothing in me to make a change, knowing in the back of mind while lying in the hospital that I had dope stashed all throughout my house and on top of that a hundred dollars. Yes, all of that was waiting for me in my room, under my bed, in my robe, and I just knew Miles wasn't going to touch it, or so I thought.

When it was time for the baby and I to leave the hospital, Miles did come and picked us up. On our way home in the car, he would hardly even speak to me as I was bitching at him. We got home, I walked into my house, opening the door in total shock of the sight from what my eyes beheld. My house was filthy. Now, even though I was using dope and all that stuff, I always kept a clean house, always. My floors would shine with such a gleam that you could see your reflection in them, but here's my house filthy and dirty from the front to the back because my man had been partying real hard while I was laid up in the hospital with our new son.

I asked him to go to the store and get some champagne so we could really celebrate. While he was gone my brother came by. I am aware that he is a crackhead; something I knew nothing about at the time but later it would be a living nightmare in which I could not be awakened from for a long period of time. No matter how much I struggled to regain consciousness of living a normal life, no matter what I seemed to do, no matter the circumstance or the situation, the nightmare that I was about to live in the crack twilight zone, the nightmare that you dream as you start to fall from the top of the cliff, the nightmare that you desperately want to awake from before you hit the bottom, the nightmare that keeps you tossing and turning afraid to drop another moment, afraid of being at the door of death, the nightmare of being addicted to crack would haunt me to the grave of death, haunt me spiritually, physically, emotionally and mentally. It would break me down to the lowest degree of human nature.

He is telling me all about my man and the treacherous life that he is leading as a drug addict. I could not believe what I was hearing. He said, "Wanda, Miles was smoking crack, snorting cocaine and hanging out with his ex-old-lady all the while you were in the hospital having the baby and he took your hundred dollars."

He's telling me about all these occurrences regarding Miles and I couldn't take it. All I could say to him was: "No, you are lying. My man wouldn't do nothing like that to me." And I told him to leave. "Go, get out." When Miles finally came home, I immediately confronted him with the allegations that my brother had informed me about and he admitted to them all. I took my engagement ring off and put it on the table.

Miles said, "Baby, don't ever smoke no crack because you'll get hooked the first time you do it." Feeling violated and betrayed, hurt, filled with anger and, at the same time, I still loved him; I just started to cry. What is it that a man can do a woman so wrong and yet she still stays with and loves him? We did not speak for the rest of the evening.

The next day, Sunday, he asked me to marry him because Monday he had to go to court for selling dope and did not know if he would make it back home because he was facing some time in the penitentiary but I was hurt and disillusioned. So, I said, "I don't know." I felt as if I had been gored with a long knife right through my heart because I believed and trusted in him and I told him, "Don't you ever hide nothing from me again. I'm your woman but more than that I'm your friend and if anything, I'm

73

your backbone and you are mine; me for you and you for me. I refuse to have people talking behind my back saying, I'm a stupid, blind bitch." He promised not to hurt me again, so we continued our relationship.

Monday came. He went to court and didn't come home. He called and asked me to go get the family reverend so that we could be married and we did, via the telephone because he was in jail but I was happy. When I got home from visiting him in jail, my sister came over to help me celebrate the occasion of being a newlywed. We had Christian Brothers Brandy, Night Train Wine, cocaine and weed. It was all the way righteous and we were doing it, man, doing it; drinking, snorting cocaine and smoking marijuana, getting high. My dream had come true; I was finally married, the wife I always wanted to be.

Well, a little later that evening, one of my girlfriends came by. She was nodding from her shot of heroin but I didn't care. I even offered her a drink and she accepted. While she was sitting there on the couch nodding, she spilt her drink on the floor, which was quite clean. I had this fetish about keeping my floors as well as my house immaculate. I kept my tables dusted and polished. Everything was in place nice and neat. I believed in making and keeping my home as my castle, no matter what it looked like on the outside, no matter if it was the projects; it was my home.

So, when this happened I started to grab the mop but I remembered that it only had three strings on it and the thought of it embarrassed me. Instead, I grabbed a newspaper that was rolled up and as I was unrolling it so that I could use it to wipe up the spill, I discovered a glass pipe; a straight shooter, an instrument used to smoke crack cocaine. My sister said, "Oh, sneeze, we gone do it now."

My girlfriend immediately came out of her nod and went to get another girl to cook the dope, the cocaine, that we were snorting. As I was watching her, she said I would have to give her some for cooking it. I said, "Okay." I didn't know what it was about then and didn't care but here it was, my wedding day, my man was in jail and hello to crack. I ended up spending a lot of money that night and really didn't even feel the full effect of crack but there was something about the feeling of smoking it that I liked and I wanted some more.

I was broke the next day and the crave was on. Mind you, now, I'm on AFDC, my husband's down (in jail) and every payday I was getting high smoking crack. It was a good thing that I was on modified payments, meaning receiving a check every two weeks, because I really would have been messed up if I would have gotten it all at once. But here I am buying crack, accepting collect calls from my husband in jail the bills were not being paid. I'm stuck on stupid.

One day I went to visit Miles in jail and he noticed that I had lost weight. I lost a lot of weight; so much so that I started wearing my son's clothes underneath my clothes to cover up my weight loss. Oh well, that was just the way it was at that time and I didn't care. I did but then again I didn't. You see when you are addicted to crack there are times when nothing else matters except smoking some more crack. Crack had become my God. Although in the back of your mind you really want to do the right thing and you want to live right and take care of your business like you are supposed to do but the psychological effect of crack has you turned inside out and you just don't care. All you live for is another hit of crack.

Years passed by, still addicted to crack and my husband was back at home from jail. We started smoking crack together, spending my welfare check, again smoking dope. He was staying out all night, wouldn't even come home to eat but he was also leaving some crack for me, some cocaine powder to snort and weed to keep me pacified and on a leash. What I mean is anyone addicted to crack can be put on leash just like a dog waiting for the master (crack) to give you a command. Just like a dog, you humbly obey; sit, stay, come, roll over, bark, beg, all in the name of crack.

On one particular occasion, and there were many, I was cleaning my house, it was at night, and I heard some voices outside. The window was open. Miles had gone to make dope sells. I went into the living room and heard a big crash. There's havoc outside and a dude says, "Hey, man, you could have hit a kid with that bottle." Another guy says, "F---you, mother f-----. I'll f---- you up. Come on, come on." I looked out the window and no one was there. So, I started cleaning and waxing my floor. A few minutes later, I heard a big BOOOM, a gunshot. I ducked and crawled straight into the bathroom and sat on the toilet for a long time.

My nerves were shot and I was scared, paranoid because I did not know what to think or what was going on. I crawled on the floor into the kids' room to look and see if they were all right; thank God they were. I crawled back into the living room, grabbed my crack, my pipe, and my alcohol, and crawled into the bathroom and sat there on the toilet seat listening. While I attempted to light my pipe, I was just shaking so badly. I couldn't even light it. So, I put it down and I'm saying to myself: "Where's Miles?" And he was nowhere to be found.

Pretty soon he came home. He walked into the house with this smile on his face. I'm thinking he is laughing at me but then again, that's how the addiction to crack can make you feel; thinking one thing is happening and in actuality it's just your mind tripping, your imagination running away. He asks me "What's up?" He says, "Everything is all right; just chill, go and take your bath." So I did and continued getting high.

Time passed and I became pregnant again. During this time I wasn't getting any medical attention, none at all. It wasn't that I didn't care about my baby to be; rather my priority was getting high, smoking crack. I remember thinking that this was the most difficult pregnancy I ever had gone through in having all of my children. I remember Miles would not even touch my stomach to feel the baby. Maybe he thought the child was not his and it wasn't. You see, during all the time he was in and out of jail, I was supporting my habit and in doing so I slept around with other guys. That too is all a part of the addiction and the scandalous life you lead living as a crackhead. So, I was not for certain whether I knew for sure that he was not the father.

76

I remember during my pregnancy that I stopped feeling the baby move inside of me but I didn't trip. This feeling came on me some time after I discovered that I was pregnant. I was still smoking crack, heavily, drinking and smoking marijuana as well as cigarettes. This I am sure were all contributing factors for me not feeling my baby during the pregnancy.

When it came time for me to deliver the baby, the doctor asked me if I was receiving any medical attention. I lied and said yes, because I did not want them to test my baby's blood for crack. I know now that I should have told the doctor the truth, that I had not received any medical attention during my pregnancy but I didn't. Upon the delivery of my baby, there was a lot of commotion going on with the doctor and the staff. I asked, "What, what's happening, what's happening with my baby? Where's my baby? I want my baby." The doctor told me to keep calm. "What's happening with my baby?" And he said to me that my baby was born stillborn; that my baby was born with his brain outside his skull; his head. I was in shock, okay, total shock, but you see when you are a drug addict, hooked and on crack, for the most part nothing else matters or rather nothing affects you that much except having another hit. He told me that the sperm did not cover the egg and that my baby's brain was exposed.

Now, the average mother would have freaked out, right? But I did not. Instead I went over to my mother's house, got myself a drink, some crack, my pipe and commenced getting high again because getting high was my priority. My mother said to me that if I kept living the life that I was leading, God would take something precious from me but I had just lost my child, my newborn baby, so there couldn't be too much more God would or could do. As a matter of fact, my response to her was: "Yeah, okay!! Whatever." And kept on hitting the pipe; one month later my mother died and what she said to me that evening had come to pass. The angle of death had taken my mother and my newborn baby. Death was becoming my best friend.

A couple of months later, Miles went to jail again. I'm still smoking crack as usual, that's the life of a drug addict; we live to use and use to live. I'm strung out and really don't give a damn. Later, Miles gets out of jail and comes to my pad; we are still together, husband and wife. During this time I stopped getting high. He tried to turn me on but I held my ground not for long but this particular time I did.

He comes by again; I have not had sex for a long, long time. I'm still not getting high, I had no desire to. As I said before I was trying to stay on the right track. I was attempting to get my life together and I started by staying clean but you cannot be truly clean unless you cut the people out of our life who are your drug friends; those who are still suffering from their own addiction getting high, smoking crack. There's just no way you can do it and if you think you can, well you are just lying to yourself.

Then one day while the kids were in school, he came by again, Miles that is. Just like the devil, he keeps coming and coming until he gets you. He had the bag of temptation in his possession; crack. The devil is always going to try and tempt you, especially when you are trying to do no wrong. He threw the drugs on the table and I didn't even want any dope in my heart, I didn't. But I was weak. So, I went and got my crack pipe—that's another thing: you've got to get rid of all your paraphernalia, everything has got to go; the pipe, the screens, the chore boy, the brillo, (tools that melt the crack allowing you to smoke it) matches, lighters, butane, alcohol, razor blades (to cut the crack), the special plate you use for that holds your crack, the metal wires you use to clean and retrieve the residue from your pipe, even your little carrying kit that keeps everything I just talked about. Everything has got to go when you finally decide to get clean, absolutely disappear because you can't fight the demon when he is there in all forms of your addiction. You must recognize it and let it all go.

Finalization was about to take place in this chapter of my life as a crack addict and I could not see it. Miles and I started getting high. As we got ready to have sex, my oldest two children came home from school. Felecia, eleven, and Carl, nine years old, but you have to understand I hadn't seen my man nor felt him inside of me for so long and I wanted him and he wanted me.

So, I fixed my boy some rice, he loved the way I cooked my rice and I was rushing to get him out of the house so we could continue doing what we wanted to do. A few minutes later, there's a knock at the door and one of my son's friends says, "Wanda, Wanda, something happened."

"What?" I exclaimed.

He said, "Carl, Carl, Carl got hit by a car."

Miles put everything down, the crack and the pipe, and rushed outside. I grabbed the younger children, took them upstairs and ran outside to the end of the building where there is a crowd of people; along with an ambulance and police cars. They are putting my baby in the ambulance with Miles. They put me in a police car. I'm crying, I said, "Why can't I be with my baby? Why do I have to ride in the police car? That's my baby, my man, my protector." I remember Carl always came to my rescue when Miles used to abuse me. He started doing this abusing and battering of me after we got married and started falling deeply into our addiction. Carl, my oldest son, was always trying to protect his mama, my man, my baby. He was always there for me through the thick and the thin, no matter what and here he was riding to the hospital in an ambulance hit by a car because I wanted to rush him out of the house to smoke more crack and have sex with my husband.

When I finally get to the hospital, I went to see my baby. They had put a needle in his head checking to see if his brain had swollen. He's lying there with black and blue eyes, face puffed up along with a broken ankle in excruciating pain. The doctor said we would have to transfer him to Kaiser Hospital because that is where I had my insurance and after all the treatments and tests, they said he would be all right. I said, "Thank God."

The next day Miles and me are getting high again smoking crack and I said I was going to see Carl at the hospital. He tried to get me to stay home and continue getting high... Wow, now that I think about it, that was absurd. I got up and threw the crack on the floor and I told him, "I'm going to see my baby with you

79

or without you." He kept on getting high smoking crack as I walked out the door going to see my son.

When I got to the hospital my son saw me as I walked into the room and said, "Hi, Mama, where's Daddy?"

I said, "Baby, he'll be here soon, how you feeling?"

He said, "Mama, take care of Velva and Little Ray."

And I said, "It's okay, baby."

He said, "Mama, I'm coming home and when I get there I ain't gonna never leave you, Mama. I ain't even gonna go outside, I'm just gonna stay in and be with you." Then he said, "Mama, my head hurts."

I got the doctor and he gave him some more pain medication through the IV he was hooked up to. He said, "Mama, it's getting dark. Daddy ain't coming. You better go home." And I did.

While riding the bus home, a lady came up to me and said, "Child, you look so said, so depressed. Here is ten dollars." And she gave me the name of a church, asked me to come by and visit or just give them a call. I took that ten dollars and bought a hit of crack cocaine.

The next day I got my AFDC check. My husband wasn't home that day nor did he come home the night before. So, I went out and spent my money on food and clothes for my kids. I felt good. My son, Carl, was coming home. As I was taking all my shopping bags into the house, a little girl came running up to me at the door and said, "Wanda, Wanda, the police came and took Miles."

I replied, "Yeah, yeah." Because I am used to the police coming and going in and out of my life always taking Miles to jail.

She said, "No, no, it's Carl, something about Carl."

I ran outside barefooted and found someone to take me to the hospital. When I got there, I walked into Carl's room and the doctor was there to greet me. He said that my boy was brain dead; that his brain had died. I ran to the bed where my son was lying and I grabbed my baby. He was on this oxygen machine and I said, "Wake up, wake up, please, just wake up."

All his friends came to the hospital the next day to see him.

The doctor told us that we had to take him off the machine and that we as the parents had to unplug it. Miles said, "I ain't gonna do it." He too was spellbound with grief and guilt and did not know how to cope or deal with this traumatic situation of death. I felt the same way but someone had to do it.

So, I did, with the help of God, who should have been my consultant all along, but...I unplugged the machine that was prolonging my nine-year-old son's life. After I did that, I reached down on the bed and took him in my arms and I held my boy, my baby, my man, I held him, I held him, I held him, and I held him and I held him until his body turned cold.

After his funeral I didn't care about my life. I even wanted to die, suicide stayed on my mind constantly. I had said more or less screw life, screw it. I had lost my two best friends whose faces I would never see on this earth again, whose embrace shall never be in this time and space, a pity, a pathetic pity.

I began using dope to no means of an end, crack, weed, alcohol, and even heroin. What was there to care for? Life had dealt me the hand of death once too many times and I was ready to fold my hand to death and, at the same time, without any hesitancy or reservations, go for myself to the grave of death that awaited me. I was heeding its call to die, heading for the call of misery, heading for the call of suffering and pain. So, getting high was all I planned to do from that moment on until the day I died.

My oldest daughter, Felecia, could not take it anymore. I very well couldn't blame her. She ran away for five years telling the Child Protection Services that I didn't buy any food, clothes, nothing; that I didn't care about her or any of my children; that my only concern in life was dope, getting high and that was oh so true. As a result, they took my children: Felecia, Velva and Little Ray.

I became pregnant again. My husband was in jail and I'm pregnant but not by him. He got out six months later and asked me to give the child up for adoption. I said, "Yes." But deep down inside I knew that was a lie. At my eighth month of pregnancy he went to jail again. Damn my life was really

81

undeniably all the way in the left lane and I kept asking God for some help and it never seemed to come but then again now that know him that is just like God. He may not come when you want him to but he is always on time.

The thought of quitting dope never crossed my mind. I mean seriously it did not. I just knew that I would continue my life as a substance abuse person until the day I would die. I knew that there was no other hope for me and I knew that deep down inside I did not want any hope. I wanted the pain and the misery, I wanted the hurt. I wanted the pity and I wanted all of it, for it was my way of escaping reality.

Then one day my brother, who had become clean and sober, mentioned The Jalani Rehabilitation Center For Women.

I said, "Yeah, okay, what about it?"

He said, "Go and check it out." So, I did.

They wanted my AFDC check for board and care expenses. I said, "Yeah, me, a crack addict, going to give all my money to you. Do I look like a fool?" I got paid the next day and spent my entire check on drugs. As I was getting high, I began to think of the idea of being clean; what a scary feeling to even try and attempt being clean after so many years of being a junkie.

But the more I thought about it, the more I was convinced that I had more to lose than to gain by staying an addict addicted to crack because that was life. In the back of my mind I always looked forward to the moment when I would not be a slave to getting high because, you see, there is always the last high, the one you've hoped and prayed for within, the one you've searched for time and time again but never seem to find. Will you make it to rescind the addiction? Who knows. The thing is: will you be alive for the next hit? I decided to check out The Jalani House.

My brother came by the following day blowing his car horn. "Hey, Wanda, you ready to go?" I went, I learned, and I prayed thanks to the Almighty goodness of God's ever loving kindness (Forgiveness), mercy (A Second Chance), and grace (Unmerited Love)... They gave me the tools to combat the forces of evil (Satan), to combat my drug addiction. I can testify today of having five years of sobriety and cleanness from drugs and alcohol.

What would my life have been if it were not for him? I shutter to think about it. Now, I'm content with my life, not always happy all the time but that's life. I plan on getting my other two children back from the Child Protection Services and have them to join my other two children who now live with me. If it be God's will, all my children will be home together again.

LETTER TO CARL

Dear Carl:

This letter is from your mother. I am writing to tell you that I am sorry for letting you go outside that day when you came home from school. This letter really hurts for me to write but I must do this to let you know and to let it go.

The day you got hit by that car, me and your dad were getting high on crack cocaine and I wanted to rush you out of the house so that we could continue getting high and have sex. I am sorry, baby, from the bottom of my heart; I am but I just had to let you know.

When you were in the hospital you asked me to get off drugs. Well, baby, it took some time but Mama is off drugs now and your sisters and brothers are back at home living with me. Felecia, Velva and Little Ray and Monique. Oh, yeah I forgot to tell you you have a little sister.

Me and your sisters and your brother are doing well. I have been off crack and alcohol for seven years now and I am now a drug counselor at The Jalani House Rehabilitation For Women.

I Love You
See Ya In Heaven One Day
Mama

ENABLERS

WHAT IS AN ENABLER? MOST OFTEN it is a family member, friend or loved one who knows that there exists a problem of drug addiction or substance abuse within a person's life and yet they, in the darkness, the shadow and deepness of their mind, know that they are contributing to the ongoing sickness of addiction and helping the one who is strung out to continue to be addicted; be it husband, wife, mother, father, sister or brother, aunt or uncle, cousin or whomever. I don't fault you whole-heartedly but think about this: I understand you would rather help them in their addiction every now and then hoping they might come out of it, or so you may think, rather than to see the one you love get into serious trouble or end up in jail. However, if you know from the pit of your soul that you are helping with the continuation of habitual drug use, I'm sorry to say; sad but true, you are not upholding in the least bit what is right. As a matter of fact, you are an enabler. In reality you are just as bad as the drug dealer or even worse because they don't care and you do. Think about it.

I understand your reasoning being: "If I give him or her

money to maintain their habit, at least they will not be out robbing, stealing, or selling their body thus keeping them out of jail." However, what you are really doing is supporting them. It's hard but that is exactly what you are doing and if you cannot or will not face that fact then all you are doing is corroborating the needs of a drug addict; bottom line.

You have got to face it, just like the crack addict has to face it. They are a junkie, sick, a crackhead; unable to come to grips that they are strung out. Some do want help, others don't want any help at all, just another hit and that is just the way it is. I know it is not a consistent (when you do what you do) type of situation, where you do it time and time again, but the times that you do makes it no better. You may think that it is better for you to give ten or twenty dollars or less or more than to have them out robbing or stealing it from someone else; in actuality, it does not make a difference.

Why? Because after they have spent the money you have given to them, they will only want more and more and more and if that is what they want, the sharing of your money will not make a difference. They are going to out and get it; more money or whatever it takes to get it (crack) come rain or shine and that's a fact.

Please, please understand this: I know it may be hard but you have got to use tough love and learn to say no, say it with love out of love. I remember when I was heavy in my drug use and I would go to my mother to get money and she knew that she was contributing to my addiction. After a long while of lying, stealing and burning the bridge that helped bring me across, she said to me: "Sink, swim or die, I am not supporting your drug habit." That message hit home. It took a long time thereafter but those words sank deep in my heart. You tell them you know what's going on and try to seek some counseling.

When they are high, keep them there with you for two to three hours because that is about how long it takes the drug to wear off and that is only temporary because it is still in their mind and that is where the control is (the mind) but at about that time maybe both you and your addicted loved one will come to terms with the reality of what's really going on and try to get some help.

This is not going to happen overnight. It is going to take some time and more time to get a grip on this individual to help them come back; that is, if they want to come back. If they do not at least you can say you tried. It's hard but it's true. Try and try again and may God forever bless you in your efforts.

YOUTH

THERE ARE SO MANY YOUNG PEOPLE every day venturing into the drug scene, traveling down the road of disillusion. Oh, it starts out as fun. It starts out as recreation. It starts out under pressures of peers. It starts usually with experimentation; a taste of alcohol and then marijuana.

Oh, oh, oh! Mera-Wanna, how I want you, I want you; want you.

Oh, oh, oh! Alcohol even more.

Alcohol, alcohol, Ho-Co-Al, I forgot; I'm drunk, is that how to spell it?

However, sometimes, and in most cases, the venture leads to the road of crack; thus getting hooked. I tell you right now, young people, the start of addiction begins when you take your first drink or your first puff and you like it. That's not to say that all young people who go down this road will be a drug addict but my advice to you is: don't take the chance. Is the risk worth the injury?

It's a crying shame to see them so young waddling in the wiles of the cesspool of drug and alcohol use. We, as a caring American culture, need to snatch them from the jaws of chemical substance abuse of crack cocaine and any other illegal drug out on the streets before they get chewed up, because that is inevitably what is going to happen. They will be chewed up and discarded like a piece of bubble gum; no flavor, no taste; good for nothing. If you have or know of any youth that are dibbling and dabbling with drugs, extend yourself to him or her immediately with love and compassion and help them as much as you possibly can to overcome their dilemma through education, wisdom, knowledge and understanding.

Many young people start out using drugs, mainly marijuana, as a recreational drug which in most senses is what it is. However, there's always someone in the group graduating to another high, a higher high thus influencing the peer pressure that they may face. The best advice I can give you personally is to not use any drug at all. Some will have to see for themselves because they already know or think they know everything but as mama used say: "Experience is the best teacher." And after you have fallen on your butt, you will know like you have never known before the pitfalls of a drug user and where it takes you, good God; straight to a living hell.

TROY

AS FAR BACK AS I CAN remember...starting out in school while living in Japan, my father was in the military and I was what they called a "military brat." Those are the children who have parents in the military and they would move their families from duty station to duty station for a certain period of time according to the orders of the government they would receive. There was nothing offensive about it that was just the way things were. I never knew prejudice or anything like that. My parents were Christians and they taught me to love everyone regardless of their race.

My best friend was this Japanese kid. We got along real good. We did a lot of things together that young boys normally do. I don't know if stealing was normal but we did that too. We pretty much had fun times as kids. I remember times when the other Japanese kids would ride by on their bicycles spitting at me and yelling bad words at me; this particular phrase they called me all the time was "baca." I think it meant stupid or something of that nature and if they called me anything other than that, I never knew it because I never knew their language.

When I was six years old we moved back to the States to the Travis Air Force Base in Fairfield, California, about 40 miles east of San Francisco. Life at that base was pretty good except for one thing. I learned the meaning of prejudice. I met some white kids there that I got along with very well but there were those who I did not get along with. This was the first time I learned of the word "nigger." But what shocked me even more was the black people. These kids had a bad attitude.

They seemed to be real violent about life; always beating up on the white kids and I did not understand this. Then there were those who would beat up on other black kids, the weaker ones like myself, taking my lunch money all the time. This one particular kid named Leroy would take my lunch money day in and day out up until the time my friend Melvin intervened and stopped him. He was like our guardian angel and he really cared about me and the weaker black kids being bullied by the likes of this shady character named Leroy. Melvin would beat up on him to stop him from doing his evil deeds.

During this time I never knew about drugs. I did not smoke or drink and I never knew any kids who did. My childhood was pretty good up until the time my dad went to Vietnam and our family moved to Arizona. That's when I came in contact with my identity and started disliking my own people. Not for what they were but more for what they stood for; prejudice. Being a loving person and getting along with everyone was just a way of life living on the Air Force bases; people were just like that. It is like you are almost forced to, but not really. We were raised like that because you always see the same people all the time and you just got along with each other.

So, I get to Tucson, Arizona, the place where I was born, and we lived in a section that was primarily where blacks and Mexicans lived. It was a ghetto and it had some very mean people. I remember being initiated into the neighborhood. There was this dog named "Wino" and the older kids would get him drunk all the time. He never messed with anyone. He was just a good dog; staggering around howling from being drunk. Anyway,

91

some kids in the neighborhood killed Wino; they cut his head off and put it on my front porch. When I went outside to put the garbage out, I saw his head and screamed. That had a very profound effect on my mind for a long time. After doing drugs for twenty-five years I still remember that incident as clear as day. I still suffer from the trauma I went through as a result of seeing that dastardly deed.

I met this kid named Charles and we became good friends. He was retarded and me, being the person that I was then, I was compassionate to Charles. We were just cool as friends. It was not because of his condition that drew me close to him but because he was not a violent or militant person. We played a lot of games together like G.I. Joe and Cowboys and Indians. It was fun having him as my friend. His brothers were just the opposite; they were violent, always into crime and doing the wrong things. They stole and beat up people in the neighborhood. There were a lot of violent episodes in my life and at school. At the age of twelve there were a lot of riots with rival turfs; the Mexicans against the blacks. This made me not want to be around black people because that was all they ever did and this was just not type of person I was raised to be.

I also learned this thing called rapping, not today's rap. Our rap was simply just talking to the girls; this was something that fascinated me because I could never do like the other guys and it was a mystery to me how these guys would get these girls, pretty girls, and I couldn't. (Back in those days you had to earn the girl's respect in order to be with her; some of the girls these days are just too easy.) Then again I was basically a shy person and I found out that these guys were telling lies to the girls just to get next to them to have sex and I was not this type of guy who could lie and be comfortable while doing it. I could never tell a girl that I loved her when I did not. It was strange to me trying to figure these things out.

One day, out of the blue, this boy named Randy, with a big Afro and modern clothes, came up to me to borrow my bike. He just looked real cool to me and not like a nerd; the way I looked.

92

I didn't even know him but he had the hairstyle of the times and that fascinated me because to wear an Afro meant something. It meant that you were part of The Black Movement, like the lyrics in the song by James Brown, "Say It Loud, I'm Black and I'm Proud." I had to get my hair cut every two weeks in a covadice style, which basically was getting all your hair cut off along the sides and the back with just little bit of hair on the top of your head. I could never wear an Afro because my parents, rather my uncle, did not think it was right to wear because it meant that you were a militant person and my people were not standing for none of that black militant stuff. I wanted to have long hair and be able to have the Jesus Christ look (man, was I brainwashed) and flick my hair around like the white boys would do.

So, I let him borrow my bike, without a second thought, mainly because he said he was going to give me five dollars for using it when he returned and that he would only be gone for an hour. He came back in two hours, minus the five dollars he promised me and as much as I can recall, I was not angry with him about it. As a matter of fact, he talked me into going up into the hills with him. This all happened while my family was stationed at Hamilton Air Force Base in Novato, California, thirty minutes north of San Francisco. That's the thing I was talking about earlier, "military brat kids"—you get to know each other as you move from base to base.

So, we go up into the hills and he pulls out some marijuana; a joint. I remember asking him what it was and got kind of paranoid because I heard that dope makes you hallucinate and see things like monsters and stuff like that but the peer pressure was on. He finally convinced me to try it and to take a hit, so, I took a hit and nothing happened for a while but I kept on smoking it with him; passing the joint back and forth and things appeared to be moving in slow motion. I was high. I saw this really big gopher snake moving on the ground and at that time I really liked snakes and frogs, lizards, guppies and all of these type of insects, reptiles and amphibians because when I was younger I collected them all the time; they fascinated me as a kid. As I went to pick up this snake, I was moving in slow motion and I just could not catch up to it because of the movement of my body. He just disappeared and that tripped me out and I just started laughing. I did not know why I was laughing. Randy started laughing too and we just kept on laughing and laughing.

After that we sat down on the hill. I was looking at these cows that were grazing in grass, they were about a football field length away and all of sudden it seemed to me that they just froze; suspended in time just like a big beautiful picture. The birds also seemed to have stopped in midair as they were flying. I knew everything that I was looking at was real but at the same time everything seemed to have stopped and posed. I enjoyed this feeling of being high; this feeling that would haunt me for the next twenty years being a drug addict. I smoked pot for a long time after that and it seemed strange to me not to. I was hooked. There was not a day that went by that I was not high.

Hanging out at this apartment was where I met a pimp for the first time in my life. I was totally impressed because I wanted to be a pimp but I never had the makeup or the personality. While we were sitting around getting high there was this dog that they had named "Sam," and these people kept Sam loaded all the time on weed mixing it in with his food. It was funny because if someone would come to the door, Sam would bark exactly three times: "Woof, woof, woof." Then he would just lay back down. Man, that was a gas.

While we were there on one occasion, and there were many but on this particular occasion, a lady come over with her baby. While we were getting high, I began to look at this baby. It was moving in slow motion and it froze just like I had seen the cows in the pasture freeze. I thought I killed the baby and I began tripping-out; shouting to everyone, "I killed the baby, I killed the baby." Everyone started laughing at me. As I looked at the baby again, it started to move. Man, what a relief that was.

Things are happening pretty much the same for me at this time smoking weed; getting high. Moving on to another episode, the next phase of my addiction was when my family moved from

Hamilton Air Force Base in Novato, California, back to Travis Air Force Base in Fairfield, California. Dad was still in the service at the time and I met this white boy named Bill who was my first real friend. I still had Randy from Hamilton who later moved to Fairfield also and all of us started hanging out together and getting high but my friend Bill was into acid, or LSD, and drinking alcohol. I was fourteen at the time, a freshman in high school and we all hung out together listening to music. Now, I liked the Motown sound; Smokey Robinson and The Miracles, The Temptations, The Supremes, Four Tops, Stevie Wonder, Martha and the Vandellas and the like. I also liked the white groups like The Doors, The Birds, The Beatles, Iron Butterfly and Led Zeppelin, to name just a few because music was my thing and if it sounded good to me then it did. There was no prejudice in me when it came to music, black or white, even jazz; that was the main music I would listen to because that was what my dad enjoyed and it transferred down to me.

As a teenager I would hear jazz greats like John Coltrane, Miles Davis, Wes Montgomery and The Jazz Crusaders. I spent many evenings at home listening to my dad and his friends having fun playing dominoes, and when I would go to bed the sound of jazz would often put me to sleep. It became an enjoyment to be a part of it.

One day we were smoking pot and Bill handed me a white tablet. I noticed that everyone else in the room was "dropping." That is what they called it then when you take pills by way of swallowing them. They asked me if I would "drop" this thing called acid. I'm thinking that acid burns because I am naïve of what it really is and, more than that, what it does to a person's mind. I did not know exactly what they were talking about but because I wanted to make friends and fit in (I always had a problem with acceptance and peer pressure). I wanted to be a part and fit in. To me the only way to be accepted with a group of people was to do what they did. So, I dropped acid for the first time.

After about forty-five minutes, the people around asked me if

I felt it and at the same time they said that it kicked in and I felt it. I felt like I was in another world and I said, "What is LSD?" I thought it was acid and then they said to me acid and LSD are one in the same and from what I had heard about LSD I knew that I was going to start tripping out.

We were watching this movie called *Picture Mommy Dead*. And there is this scene when this woman hides a very expensive necklace inside a doll and gives it to her daughter. As the movie continues this bird, a falcon, flies through the window and snatches the doll from the girl. At that time I saw the falcon fly through the television set. It was flying over my head and I started ducking and moving, trying to stay out of this bird's path. Everyone was asking me what was I doing; and then I told them. At first I was scared, then it all became a joke and we all had a good hard laugh as we were tripping on LSD; insanity had just begun to set in on my life as a drug addict.

I got used to taking acid on a regular basis and for a while. When I took it everything just seemed to be funny. I could see a spot of oil on the ground and it would turn into little roaches moving around and I would just start to laugh. My fascination for drugs was "Right On." It was just fun to me. However, the nightmare was just beginning. The nightmare that I desperately tried to wake up from many a days and many a nights; you know the nightmare, the dream when someone is chasing you, or the one when you fall from a bridge and are about to hit the water at the bottom, the one where you are about to die and you desperately struggle; trying to wake yourself from your sleep. Well, I was actually living this nightmare and waking up was even harder than when I was asleep. I guess the difference was when you sleep, you have no control but yet when I was awake in this nightmare, I still had no control.

Man, I was just starting out on the brink of insanity without any realization. That's when my friend Randy moved from Hamilton Air Force Base in Novato to Travis Air Force Base in Fairfield. We ended up being druggies together and at the same time I began to accept myself as black person and I started trying to be black. That is weird; trying to be something that you already are but you do not know it and yet you really are not. I was living a masquerade, trying to find my identity and myself in the parade of life, where everyone is wearing their own costume designed to fit their being. You just never know what the real face is behind the mask or is it the real face of the mask that you really see?

I still hung out with my white friends because when it came to drinking and partying with the white folks that is where I wanted to be. Commencing to drink wine at the age of fourteen, ultimately, the inevitable happened; I became an alcoholic. I would just drink and drink and drink. Whatever anyone else did I was going to do that and then do it one step better and I did; dropping acid, smoking weed and drinking.

One day we dropped some orange sunshine (acid) and it kept me up all day and all night tripping at my friend's mother's house. I was looking at this picture that was filled with trees and all of a sudden they just started to bend and sway like I was really in the outdoors, that was a trip, and again I just started to laugh. We went outside just standing around and my friend lay down on the grass. Without any warning he jumped up screaming and started to run; so I started to run. We ran for a little while then we stopped and just started laughing again. Man, we were really tripping.

From acid I went to taking "reds." We called them downers, because they would make you feel like you were drunk. There were also M&Ms and Thorzine and all kind of downers. I would take them just to get high; to me they were like getting drunk without the hangover. I really enjoyed this, believe it or not, along with drinking alcohol I stayed messed up. Drugs and drinking went hand in hand with me.

I was hanging out in Vacaville, California, fifteen miles east from Fairfield, with this Mexican guy named Manual. This is where a lot of white people used to go and party and that is where I went. Wherever the dope was so was I. Anyway, Manual had eight reds. We took four each and I really was not that loaded. We were just hanging out in the park enjoying our high and

Manual said he wanted to get some more. I said, "Whatever, I'm feeling good but I can feel better." So, he went and got some more and we took four each again. We both have now taken a total of eight. Now, I'm really loaded. I started to stagger around, almost seeing double, squinting my eyes just to see straight. We began to walk through the park and came upon these guys, I think it must have been two or three. I cannot quite remember. Manual started kicking one of these dudes for no apparent reason at all. I pulled him off and asked why was he doing this and he said he just didn't like the guy. Then he said he wanted to get some more reds and I said, "Whoa." This time I kind of protested because I am already really high. I said, "What the heck?" And I took them anyway. Now, we have taken a total of twelve pills each. I begin to start seeing double; I could barely even talk. Man, I was stoned out of mind and somehow we split up going in different directions.

Later on I found out he had passed out in front of a biker bar and the ambulance had to come and pick him up and take him to the hospital to get his stomach pumped. I ended up walking in the park on this wall and I fell hitting the cement. I remember feeling the pain all through my body but I couldn't move; I just couldn't. As I was lying there, I was so tired, so tired and I wanted to just go to sleep and not wake up. Actually, I was in an acute overdose stage poisoned by the intake of too many pills.

The next thing I know a van pulls up alongside of me and these white people get out, pick me up and drove off. While I was in the van riding, I kept saying: "I'm so tired, so tired. I'm tired of breathing."

I heard someone say, "No, you have to breathe, keep breathing."

I awaken in a dream-like state in a bathtub full of cold water. It was so cold, almost freezing, yet I could not get up and get out of it. I looked around at the time and these two white girls were there and everybody was talking to me telling me to wake up. I guess I was passing in and out of consciousness; I didn't know. I was too high to know anything. This one particular girl passed me something and said to me: "Here, take this." Later on I found out it was mescaline. She said this would wake me up and I said, "Okay, it's dope, so what the heck."

After that I remember going to bed with this girl, climbing on top of her, but I must have passed out. The next thing I knew, when I woke up everyone was gone. This happened on a Sunday evening and I was supposed to have been on restriction at the time but being a dope addict, I did not care about rules or regulations, only the next chance to get high. Anyway, when I finally woke up, it was Wednesday morning. I was knocked out for four days. I went into the kitchen made a peanut butter and jelly sandwich and went home.

It's almost graduation time now. At the age of seventeen, during the Superfly era when I was really trying to be black, I was introduced to crank, speed, methamphetamine. One of my friends' brothers used to shoot crank all the time and being a dope addict already, naturally I got talked into shooting up. I was really scared at first because the needle frightened me but like I said before, the only way I felt I was going to be accepted was to do what my friends did. I really did want to be accepted by my black friends, because I was desperately trying to fit in and be black and these guys were what I always wanted to be inside but never could get to it. To be a gangster type of person like Frank Nitti and Al Capone. I identified with these characters but I never could be really one of them deep in my heart. I wanted to be a part of that image; the dress, the machismo, the women, the attitude and everything that went along with that. Thank God I never ended up like that. Being a drug addict was not too much better.

So, I let this dude shoot me up with the dope. I couldn't even look at him while he was doing it. I remember asking him: "When are you going to put the needle in my arm?" not knowing that he had already done it. He was that smooth. I started to feel it from the bottom of my toes to the top of my head. I remember feeling this feel that I could run and run and run forever and I just started talking and talking; my rap was on.

We went to this party and I just started rapping to all the women; me this shy guy rapping from here to eternity. I started romancing the euphoria of crank; the feeling it gave me, the rush, the high, everything about it. This is where my insanity was starting to set in even deeper because I could not stop myself from using. My motive was simple; it was fun getting high and I enjoyed it. I kept on shooting dope even though I did not know the first thing about it. Rendering my body and soul through the addiction of crank (methamphetamine) did not get any better. As time passed on...I can recall this particular episode at the beginning of my addiction that was so repulsive, I wanted to quit but like I said before I was having fun.

Me and a friend were on our way to a party in Sacramento (that's ninety miles east of San Francisco), and as we began to shoot up the needle broke. I mean, the syringe busted right off the needle while it was in my friend's arm and he was still shooting up. Blood started squirting all over the place on him and me and throughout the car as we were riding to our destination. He took the needle out of his arm and tried one of the most bizarre things I had ever seen; he tried to fix the needle so that he could continue to shoot some more dope.

Man, it was disgusting. He even tried putting tape around it. I was not about to try and use that same needle in my arm. It's a miracle that during this time I did not come in contact with any disease leading to AIDS. I was lost on the road of addiction and did not know at this time that it had only just begun. Arriving in Sacramento, we got another needle from someone else and commenced in the act of shooting up. To me this was neither insane nor stupid at the time but rather it was just a normal way of life. And that's the way it is for people who are addicted; it's normal. Little did I know at that time that I was an addict; addicted to chemical substance dependency.

Beginning to tire of being a victim of people shooting dope into my veins because I had to share my dope for the act of their open-heartedness and turn them on for their good deed. We had this one guy that we called "The Doctor" because he knew where

100

to put the needle in your arm, finding a vein so that the dope could rush straight into your bloodstream. I hated going to "The Doctor" because that meant he got some of my dope and at this point greediness was my priority. I wanted all my dope for myself. That's how it is being a junkie; you want everything for yourself. Damn being generous; it was dog-eat-dog.

So, I started shooting up myself. I don't remember how I learned to do it but I guess when you become an addict, you overcome so many fears yet taking on new fears such as being scared of reality and living life on a normal everyday basis like most other human beings, or do they? I could not go out to a club or a party without being drunk or loaded on dope and making a total ass of myself most of those times. If I drank, normally I would pass out. I was known for passing out at parties. On the other hand, if I did too many drugs paranoia would take precedence so I would just leave the party and go do more drugs to get higher.

I could not go to a club without being drunk in order to enjoy myself and dance. I had this incredible fear about dancing. However, if I was drunk you could not even get me off the floor and if a lady would not dance with me it didn't matter; I would dance with a pole, the refrigerator or any other inanimate object as long as I was dancing. I was cool like that.

After I finally learned how to shoot myself up with dope, I got a brand-new needle but I had no dope. I desperately wanted to shoot some dope to try out my new needle. I was like a kid on Christmas Day with a brand-new toy; totally crazy but here I am with a new syringe and no money to buy no dope. *Wait a minute*, I thought and remembered I had about five dollars. I really wanted some dope so bad that I could just taste it. I had a baggie that did not even have enough crank in it to tickle my nose; however, I put some water in the baggie and mixed the miniscule amount of dope I did have and shot it not my vein. Understand this: it was not about the dope at this point or even getting high; it was all about the needle I had wanted to try out. The point at the edge of the vein, the smoothness, the feeling of it penetrating

101

into my skin, the ecstasy that it brought was almost just as good as an orgasm. In essence all I did was shoot some water into my veins, that's all it was. I imagined myself getting high off the penetration of the needle in my arm but that did not satisfy me, so my insanity went a little further; one step beyond.

Since I could not get any dope, I went to the store and bought some alcohol so I could shoot it and that is exactly what I did. I bought some Boones Farm Wine. It burnt going into my bloodstream but I did not care. I got a little buzz from this endeavor but it was not enough to satisfy the urge of the needle in my skin. So, I got some Vodka, rather I had someone else buy me some Vodka because I was still a minor, only seventeen, and could not buy any alcohol myself. I shot it up and it really burnt going into my bloodstream. I could feel the effect of it and I actually got drunk. But I wanted some dope, some real dope and I wanted it right then and there.

Funny, but I don't remember if I actually got any crank to shoot up that day. Graduation had come to pass and shooting crank into my veins stayed with me many years. I even tried heroin at one time but I don't remember too much about that.

At eighteen I joined the service, the Air Force, because I got busted for possession of a gram of crank and a big bag of weed at Fairfield High School with a minor who was fourteen years old. We got into a car that was in the parking lot not caring who it belonged to, we just wanted to find a place to smoke our dope.

When I went to court the judge dropped my charges from a felony to a misdemeanor. I asked him if my record could be sealed if I joined the service. He agreed as long as I went to the induction center as soon as I left his courtroom and I did.

Upon my arrival at boot camp, I saw a friend who I knew from high school and he brought a bag of weed with him to basic training. I continued on getting high and drinking alcohol all throughout my entire stitch while in the service. One night I had Fire Watch Duty which meant that I was supposed to stand guard for two hours. However, on this particular night I forgot about my assignment. I was out on liberty drinking Thunderbird Wine getting drunk and by time I remembered that I had guard duty, I was plastered. I could only stand up for about ten minutes and then I passed out. The next thing I remember was lying on a cot being screamed at by three or four drill sergeants; they were yelling and cursing at me and saying all kinds of derogatory statements. My punishment was pulling extra duty for a while. This was one of the many episodes of my downfall during the chemical dependency stage of my life.

While in the service I met this woman whom I ended up marrying later on. I was drinking a lot at this time and she was doing beanies, or as we would call the cross tops; a pill that keeps you wired for a long time. She had a bunch of them. During the time we were dating, she introduced me to her friend and I ended up having sex with her friend as well as with her. I met her friend's husband, who ran a pet shop, and all four of us would do drugs and end up sleeping in this pet store because we did not have anywhere to lay our bodies down; so this was the place. I had gotten out of the service on a dishonorable discharge for not performing and living up to my duties as a soldier.

He eventually found out that I was messing around with his wife and he kicked me and my wife out on the streets. She was pregnant from her first boyfriend, which did not make matters any better. I ended up staying with her. She got on welfare and things started getting real bad for us during our drug use. The food stamps that we were getting did not last long because we traded them for drugs. We would end going downtown in New Hampshire standing in front of this pizza shop watching people eat and trying to get them to sympathize with our predicament and most of the time it would work.

These people would look at us and get so sick and tired of looking that they would buy us pizza, or the people who worked there would give us a pizza. I hope God has blessed those people during their lives because at that time we were really hungry. We met a Christian and he gave us five dollars each to help us out. No, during this time, I was not a full-fledged Christian as I am today. I knew Christ but I had not dedicated my life to him because I was too busy staying high and getting drunk. My wife and I ended up separating and eventually divorced. She ended up with another man who as a good friend of mine, rather a snake who stole my woman, but in the world of drug users there are no real friends except the next of your drug. I lived on the streets a little while longer by myself before calling my parents and asking them to send me a plane ticket to come back home to Fairfield and they did.

I ran into one my old friends whom I had known from high school and we started clicking together, drinking alcohol. Since I was already an alcoholic, this fit right into my program. We began doing a lot of things as friends; going places, parties and just hanging out. Recalling one occasion when we were together. Me, him and his girlfriend, we were all drunk but I was the most drunken sober one who could drive; if that makes any sense. I kept falling asleep and waking up while I was driving. Every time I woke up, I was still in the lane that I was driving in. I was truly blessed then to make it back home that night with my extremities in tack as well as my life.

But there was another time when we all went out again. This time we were driving somewhere out in the country and all I could remember is that I was so drunk. That night I drank a fifth of Thunderbird, three cans of Old English Malt Liquor, and a bottle of Cold Duck Champagne all by myself; it just wiped me out along with some weed that we smoked. Anyway, my friend's girlfriend was driving. He was up in front with her and I was in back and all I remember was seeing a tree coming toward us at fifty miles per hour. Before I could say anything—Bam!

We hit the tree and the next thing I remember was everything starting to come into view. First it was all black and then a picture beheld my eyes. Here I am standing somewhere in the woods. The car is gone and they are too. I did not see anyone else around. Feeling like I was in the Twilight Zone, I was in the car one moment and the next moment I'm standing in the middle of a forest. As I stood there, I began to feel the warmness of blood running down my leg. I looked down and my pants were soaked in blood.

104

I was still trying to figure out what had happened, and then it occurred to me; I was in a car and my friends were nowhere to be found. How did I get to where I was? I began looking for the car. When I found it, it was empty. They were gone and this really had me confounded. I thought that I had died and was walking around as a spirit, a ghost. The windshield on the passenger side was cracked and I assumed that my friend had hit his head on the windshield. The rearview mirror was gone and the engine was protruding through the dashboard. I began panicking; then the police showed up and put me in handcuffs, telling me that I was under arrest for disorderly conduct. I had not done a thing. Here I was bleeding and now I was under arrest.

They took me to the hospital. I got checked for my injuries and was released; thinking my next ride would be to jail but they let me go home. Later, I found out that my friends were taken to the hospital by an ambulance and what a relief that was for me. Another episode of total irresponsibility being addicted to a chemical substance.

I met another friend from school who used to be in my band class, one who used to get high with me in the back of the classroom. I did not know at the time what he was really into but it came to pass that he was smoking crack cocaine; the rock and shooting up dope (crank/speed). We would shoot up together quite a bit.

Anyway, we started smoking crack together and this was the most scariest and tumultuous episode during my drug addiction. The paranoia I used to feel was unbelievable; yet I continued smoking crack rocks. I remember this one time we bought a sixty dollar rock, which was pretty big, about two grams of cocaine rocked into crack. We went to this guy's house to smoke our dope and the house rule, as in every dope house, was that you always serve the houseman first. So, we broke him off some of the dope and he pulled out his pipe, put the dope on the screen, and took a big hit and exhaled.

After that he immediately jumped up, looked at us, picked up the rock, and walked out of the room. I heard him closing the blinds, checking the locks on the doors, turning off the music, the television and everything that was plugged in that made the least bit of noise, even the refrigerator. Tweaking, he just kept running back and forth. He finally came back into the room and said, "I'm sorry." We asked him to put the rock back on the table because we wanted to get our hits too and he told us he swallowed it.

I could not believe it. Then he asked us to leave and that's the type of scandalous thing a lot people do who are addicted to crack. There is so much to this roller coaster ride of crack that I cannot even remember everything but I'll tell you the most that I do recall and hope that someone will understand or come to know the addiction of crack cocaine. What you go through while being addicted is nothing nice.

Well, Ray and I became crack monsters from 1971 to 1981 and from 1986 to 1991 and we did a lot of things out of the ordinary, totally abnormal, just to get high off crack; the rock. I still see him from time to time but he is not a Christian and he denounced God to my face and I don't care to talk to him or be in his company anymore after he made that statement.

My recollection to that event was that I called him on the phone one day and told him the good news that I had been to a drug rehabilitation program that had a Christian format and that I was saved and no longer needed drugs in my life because I had given my life to Christ.

He said, "Since you are a Christian and you believe in God and I don't, we can't be friends anymore."

I said, "I was hoping to get you to see the light."

He said, "What would it take for you not to talk to me anymore?"

And I said, "Why would you want to do that?"

He said, "I just want to know, since you are a Christian now; what would it take?"

And I said, "Well, what would it take would be for you to curse God." I couldn't think of anything else that would have been detrimental to our friendship and at that point of our conversation.

He said, "F--- God."

I said, "Oh, well, we just can't be friends."

Before all of this happened, Ray and I smoked crack for a long time, as well as shooting up, dropping acid, drinking alcohol and smoking weed. We were crankster gangsters together. Things started really getting crazy. Our addiction was so strong and intense that we wanted to smoke crack every day. Sometimes we would run out of money, so we would steal empty beer keggers from behind the place where he worked and sell them to other liquor stores for fifteen or twenty dollars each, and then we would go buy our crack at the Crest in Vallejo, California, because I knew a lot of people there and that's where the crack was at.

This went on for a while and not too long after that I lost my job. Actually I had to quit because I couldn't take it anymore. I would go to work with my dope, go into the bathroom and take a hit. I was just doing crazy stupid stuff like that all the time in the name of crack. I would call in sick and was constantly late for work. Man, it just got so pathetic that I could not even function as a normal person, but then again I was not normal at all. Finally, I did not want to deal with the job anymore so I just quit.

I moved back home with my mom and dad. While they were on vacation in Texas, Ray come by our house. At this time he was living in his car because his girlfriend had kicked him out of the house because of his addiction. He still had his janitorial job on the base where he would clean this nightclub and I had a job cleaning another club which was also on the base. I remember that we used to sneak back into the club around 2:30 a.m., after it was closed, and drink the beer and wine; just getting drunk and if we had some crack we would smoke it too. When we ran out of crack and wanted some more, we would go dumpster diving, scavenging for food the clubs used to throw out because it had expired. We would get the food and what we did not eat, we sold or traded for crack. By now my addiction as well as his was getting all the way beyond insane.

I told myself many a day that if I ever would steal from my family to get crack, then at that point I was really going to need some help. It happened. I stole from my family. My mom had this portable television set in her bedroom and I kept looking at it, debating whether or not I should take it. I did not want to take anything big or noticeable. I figured they wouldn't notice the television being gone, as if it was not a thing that she would miss. That is how stuck on stupid I was. I finally made the decision to do it and I took the television set and sold it for crack. All I got was a fifteen dollar tiny rock of crack and smoked it. All I could do after smoking the little amount of crack was to sit there and absorb the guilt and shame of what I had done—for fifteen dollars. Things were really getting bad for me and I knew I had a serious problem but yet the rock kept calling me and I answered the call time after time after time, again and again.

Shortly after this happened, I ran into Ray again. He was sitting in his car, his home, and when I looked at him (at this time I was not high) it frightened me so bad because he looked like death. I saw death on his face and I told him that we really needed to talk about our addiction and the insane things that we were doing and that it had just gone too far.

We talked about our predicament and what would help us solve our problem. We decided to go into a program of rehabilitation for drug addicts because we could not keep living the way we were living. So, we went to Martinez, California, thirty miles northwest of Fairfield, sixty miles from San Francisco. We tried to check ourselves into a rehab program there and they told us that the only program we could get into would be two weeks away and that it was located in Menlo Park, thirty miles south of San Francisco. That was a little too close to home for me because if I still wanted to get a hold of some drugs, some crack, it would be no problem. I was trying to run away from my addiction to another geographical location. As a matter of fact, I could not run. Wherever you go, you cannot run from or hide from yourself and if you are an addict and you want to use, you will find a way and you will find the spot no matter where you are, you can and you will find the spot where the drugs are sold and continue in your addiction.

In essence, that is what I really wanted; more drugs, more crack. I was not ready to quit even though I told myself that I was ready, deep in my heart I was not finished but I was trying. Plus, waiting for two weeks was like suicide for us, being drug addicts, because we knew that we were living for this crack that it was only a matter of time before destruction or death would take over completely.

Ray called his father in San Bernardino to send him some money for bus fare so that he could check himself into a program. His father accompanied his son's request and sent him sixty dollars. He bought some more crack and we smoked it up. Things were getting crazy again. Ray sold his car for a hundred dollars worth of crack and we smoked that up also in a matter of a couple of hours and we still were not satisfied. You are never satisfied smoking crack because there is never enough, never. We went back to the guy Ray sold his car to for some more dope because he owed him another twenty-five dollars and he would not give it to him. So, Ray called the police and reported his car stolen and they came and found some dope in it and impounded it. So, now we are desperately thinking that we need help and that we've got to get into a program but a program cannot help you unless you are really ready to surrender. You can go there and get all the tools that can help you to surrender but unless you really want to quit; no program on God's green earth is going to help you.

Anyway, Ray called his brother in San Bernardino and asked him to send him some money so that he could get into a program. His brother also accompanied him and we spent that money also smoking crack. We are now insane; have been but now we realize it; rather, we are facing it—without any denial.

We were out of our minds addicted to crack. So, Ray called his father again but this time his father did not send him any money, rather he sent him a bus ticket and I was left out because he did not send one for me. Ray left and now here I am still strung out trying to feed my habit yet trying to give it up. Then something happened. I don't know how to explain it but for some strange reason God came and intervened. Out of the blue a friend of mine just popped up from Reno, Nevada. A friend who I used to party and get high with and he told me that he did not get high anymore and rarely ever drank.

I told him about my problem and he invited me to come live with him in Reno. He said he would work with me, get me into a recovery program. I packed my things and went to Reno and stayed with him about a month. It was a living hell because every day I wanted to get high so bad and I could not get a hold of any dope so I drank and I drank as much as I could drink, trying to relieve the pressure of getting high, now knowing that all I was doing was contributing even more to my chemical dependency. I called my parents from Reno and told them what my plans were. I apologized to my mother for stealing her television and I told her that I would buy her another one—something I still have to do. My parents said that they, as well as the church members at our church, were praying for me during this trying time. I asked her not to send me any money only a bus ticket; that I was going to go to San Bernardino, where my friend Ray was and go to the same program which he was already in.

My first stop on the bus was in Sacramento and my addiction was calling me again, but I told myself that I have to have this last drink and boy did I. My parents sent me sixteen dollars for food along with the bus ticket and I did buy food but I bought some booze too for the last binge. When I arrived in San Bernardino, it was early in the morning and I wanted one last drink before I went to the hospital. Fortunately, and this is where God stepped in again, I did not get that drink because all the stores were closed and I did not have enough time to wait for a liquor store to open because the bus was leaving. So, when I got to the hospital they could not register me right away but they let me stay in one of their recovery homes for the night. The next day I checked into the hospital and I met a minister named Bruce, he was also a counselor on the ward. He talked to me and asked me if I have ever been saved and I told him no, and he asked if I wanted to know Jesus and I said, "Yes." I never did stop believing in God.

I just never accepted him into my life.

Minister Bruce prayed for me that day and after that God just touched my heart and I never wanted to do drugs or drink again. This was the first Christmas and New Year's that I had without drugs or alcohol and I cried and I cried and I cried because it hurt so bad that I could not be at home with my family and I was not used to this but there were so many people there who loved and helped me, while Minister Bruce continued to pray for me.

I went into a recovery home after being in the hospital and Minister Bruce would come by and pick me up, and anyone else who wanted to go to church, and I felt so much love from the pastor and the entire congregation. God just changed my heart from that moment on. All I wanted to do from that day on was to witness and tell people how God was so good and how he delivered me from my addiction. For those addicts who are still suffering...I am here to tell you that God is real and it's the best thing in the world to be free and saved by his grace.

So, you who are still struggling and trying to come back, all I want to tell is this: try God. I mean, you tried everything else, why not give him a chance? Let Jesus come into your heart and deliver you like he delivered me. And for those people young or old who think they might want do it—try crack or any other drug and become a drug addict—don't. All I've got to say to you is: DON'T DO IT, because if you do, surely you will live to see the day, or maybe you won't, that you will regret that you ever tried crack. Believe you me, it's true. I know, I lived it and I don't want to live like that ever again.

Drugs are nothing but the devil, they are no good and you will never have a good life with drugs as you co-pilot, you will never make it to heaven and you will never know the love of Jesus. I am telling you firsthand that it is a love you never ever want to lose because it will just break your heart, to lose the love of Jesus which at the same time you can never lose because he will always forgive you.

I hope my story will help save someone from going over the edge or bring someone back.

God bless you.

RELAPSE

THE RELAPSE SYNDROME IS VERY DEEP but to pick up and use again is giving yourself a death sentence. The only difference between death row and death by relapse is that on death row you know your scheduled date to die. When you relapse you are now walking dead. Oh! I should not be so dramatic with this issue but it behooves me to have conquered my addiction through my program which is God and to forfeit all of my clean and sober time to use again.

This subject is very sensitive. I relapsed at least three times before I got completely clean and now I know that I'll never be completely clean and sober. Why? Because I know the feeling of getting high from smoking crack and drinking alcohol. It's a feeling that a person will not forget. Look at it like this you have a child and your child dies. You bury your child but the feelings of knowing and having felt from your child will never leave. So, you still have got to on and live your life and let live, let die.

In order not to relapse some precautions must be taken and taken very seriously; that is, if you want to stay clean. The absolute first thing you must do is to admit that you are an addict, in doing so you give yourself a fighting chance to not pick up and use or even better yet; follow the steps of the Big Book. (Alcohol/Narcotic Anonymous); anything that will help you not to use. After admitting to yourself that you are a crackhead…ooo that sounds so disturbing, doesn't it? Well, it's true. So, after you have admitted to yourself who you are and what you are, you can now begin the process of rebuilding; just make it to the page where you are a sinner saved by grace; that's not in the Big Book. Now that you have made your admission the work begins, the real work because relapse happens long before you actually pick up and use. It is almost impossible once you are an addict not to relapse—not an impossibility but almost. You can make it if you sincerely try. The first thing you have to do is get rid of all your paraphernalia, including money which is and can be a big setup for immediate relapse. Everything has to go. Cool, now we're working. The next thing that has to go is your friends, your drug associates. This is a matter of a fact; you cannot and will not stay clean if you hang out with other drug addicts, there is just no way, the temptation is too strong and sooner or later you will relapse; be it mother, father, sister, brother, uncle, aunt, cousin, husband or wife. You have to get in another circle of people who are clean and sober and the best people to be around are those who go to meetings and church. You need to do this for at least the first year. It's up to you, how bad do you want to be clean?

There are exceptions to the rule and that is only that you know you better than I know you or anyone else. So, I'm speaking of what works for me just might not work for you. Maybe you are an individual who can deal with the same people and stay clean. I can't and not many of you can either. The exception that I am speaking of is this; I have witnessed people who have put down the pipe and have a drink now and then and still will not pick up the pipe and that's how strong their will is and that is the whole ball of wax in a nutshell. How strong is your will?

Now, the question comes to mind: why does a person relapse? A drug dealer whom I know said to me: "Man, if you could figure out why a person would relapse, you can help a lot of people." As

I begin to think deep about the subject, I have surmised my thoughts and came to this one conclusion regarding relapsing, and this does not relate just to crack; it relates to any drug or any chemical substance that can alter your thinking and behavior after using for such a long extended period of time. So, here is my analysis on the subject: a person relapses before they relapse; meaning this, you actually set yourself up to relapse and you do this in your mind as you think. The Word clearly states so "As man thinketh so is he." I remember when I got out of rehab and I knew I had it made and I did for a while, the only problem was that while I had it made, I did not lose my association in the streets with the people in the drug world. Even though I was clean, I still lingered in the mists of their company; not directly rather indirectly. You know, walking in the neighborhood, going to the store, seeing the exchange of dope and money. All of these were contributing factors to relapse, and the worse one of all—and this is so stupid that I have to laugh—is going to the drug house and hanging out trying to prove that you have everything in control.

Oh, you just might but, believe you me, someone is going to offer you a hit one day and you will take it because you have set yourself up for the big fall. I remember walking down the street and I was clean for about a month or six weeks and I thought I had it going on. I saw one of the guys from the neighborhood buy some dope, some crack. We begin to walk down the street together; I was coming from the store. (A nice place to be set up again.) I said, "Man, I'm clean but just let me see how big a piece you got for your twenty dollars." He opened his hand and I looked at that crack rock and I kept on walking and did not relapse that day. About a week later I did because what I found out was the image of that rock in his hand stayed on mind (in the back) and as soon as I gave myself the opportunity, or rather the excuse to use, I went around the corner and bought some crack.

At the outset when you first get clean as a rule you cannot hang out with the people who are still using and when you do congregate with people who use or do not use crack, don't share your crack war stories. This is the first and most dangerous part of the relapse syndrome; rehashing or reliving the stories about getting high, how it made you feel, what you did when you did get high, how much dope you used to smoke, how many parties you had and all the things that went on at the parties, all the Sodom and Gomorrah episodes of sin you dwelt in. You must let all of that go and try not to bring them to surface again. It's like when you have lost a loved one (notice *a loved one*—past tense) through death. You cannot forget them but you don't glorify them in their grave too often unless they have left a legacy. With crack the only legacy is misery and pain, that sums it up without elaborating.

When you do speak of crack, only speak of it in terms of what it has done to you in the negative sense and how it has destroyed your life, up to now this present moment; how it has kept your soul captured in its bondage and how you became a demon for Satan because of its possession. The only war stories you should remember and exchange about crack is to tell someone else who has never been there why they don't want to ever go there. Besides, how can you glorify something that has virtually destroyed your human existence? That is what crack has done for you. Whenever you are speaking to someone about crack, get sad, get angry, get upset, start to cry, feel all of those feelings like you have never felt them before knowing exactly what this demonic destructive substance has done to you and your life. There is absolutely nothing to talk about regarding crack that is positive and if so you are only glorifying SIN; because if you smoke crack you think evil, maybe not at the outset but eventually evil comes to the forefront of your mind.

Relapse is nothing nice. It's like a dog returning to its own vomit and licking it up, and you know what happens to the dog; he gets sick again—this time worse. If a person gets clean and sober, you've got to stay clean and sober because I guarantee you this: if you pick up and use again, you will use even deeper than you did before and you will sink deeper than you ever have. But the one thing about relapsing is this: the only time a person relapses and decides to use is when they have made a conscious decision to do so. Don't be a fool (again).

THE FUNCTIONAL ADDICT

WHAT DO WE HAVE HERE? AH! Be not dismayed, these are the people who are like the chameleon changing colors, different shades of red, blue and green; looking real good on the outside but hiding what they really are on the inside; pretending that they are something they're not; a drug addict. Notice I did not say a crack addict but a drug addict. These people are not necessarily hooked on crack, could be crank, heroin, prescription drugs, alcohol, any chemical substance, but I am primarily referring to crack.

Word to the functioning addict and the word is this: you are an addict, believe it or not you are; just as I was and still am if I surrender my will. I say this to myself, to make me remember that I am not so secure that it cannot happen to me again. I was a functioning addict. What, you say, is a functioning addict? This is the person who dresses well, looks good, drives a nice car, has a nice house and is kept well from his or her head to toe. This is the person who is deceiving everyone around them when in actuality they are only deceiving themselves.

You are the ones who are in deep heavy denial, or maybe you

116

are not, depending on the person, because you still function doing the normal things that normal people do but normal people are not drug addicts, are they? And if they are, what makes them not normal? It's only a matter of opinion and you know what they say about opinions, right?

I'm not being condescending when speaking of the functional addict because I cannot any longer be a functioning addict. It's like alcohol; some people can take a drink and be done with it and some can't. It's the same thing with crack, but these people, they know their limitations. But be very careful not to slip into overconfidence because the boogie man can get you too. I have witnessed for myself the downfall of people who are functional addicts. They keep everything together as far as paying their bills and going to work on time every day; doing the right thing as far as the public eye can see. But it's within the walls of their homes, within the walls of their mind, that the demon comes out. Oh, if walls could talk what a story they would tell. Well, the wall that separates the hallways of your mind is transparent, it is a glass house. The only difference is the circumference and the thickness of the glass. Some walls are so wide, you can't get around them; some are so dense you can't break them. The walls of addiction that only the addict knows but I beg to differ, there is one that knows it all and that one is God and the other one is Satan. The prince of darkness; the one who keeps you in bondage whipping you into submission of your mind; oh what can free me from this body of death? Yes, you too are going to die in your addiction, or not. But you are going to die then you will answer to the call of your deception of life you have lived. Beware.

REA

HI, MY NAME IS REA. I am a forty-year-old white female who would like to share her story with you in relation to drug addiction. It has taken me a long time to get down and turn this tape recorder on and share my life and thoughts with you. I love people and I talk all the time. However, turning back to this chapter in my life is kind of hard to talk about. I guess I will start with where I am at today, which is at a residential program for women called The Jalani House. I am very grateful to be here. Today my life is full of hope. I am an optimist on most days with a very busy schedule. I look forward to living my life on life's terms and I know it is not going to be an easy road but I have finally surrendered my soul to take the plunge in the clean and sober lane of life, with my head to the sky and my soul and spirit to the Lord.

The program that I am in is very simple but oftentimes I find it hard work; to face the truth about yourself especially when you have been out of touch with reality and in heavy denial regarding your own drug addiction; living in a dysfunctional state of mind. I'll start from the beginning. Here goes.

I was born and lived in upstate New York; with Irish Catholic parents. I would say we were considered lower middle-class people. I am one of eight children, the second to the oldest. My earliest childhood memories are happy ones; mostly of my dad and his influence in our lives as children. My mother's memories are really distant, at least until I got to elementary school. For some reason I cannot remember her that well or rather only as an occasional picture that comes to mind. We owned a large six bedroom house in a small town called Mahopac. We were a very respectable family in our little town where everyone knew each other. My dad was a high-school football coach, and a teacher. My mother was a stay-at-home housewife.

Childhood was relatively happy and carefree; lots of nature and just hanging outdoors, with tons of Walt Disney enabling me to fairy-tale every situation. I even believed in Santa Claus until it was absolutely embarrassing to do so. I guess I was always inclined towards being tomboyish; always climbing trees, playing touch football with the boys and hanging out with Steve, my older brother.

I was a Howdy Doodie-looking little girl with a million freckles I hated but they seemed to identify me as a character. Kids would tease me. "Hey, freckles. Where did you get all those freckles?" School was the only real place we had to socialize in Mohopac since it was a spread-out countryside community. I never seemed to be in sync with my friends; their hairstyles or wardrobes since my mom was in charge of all my decisions regarding those things. I always felt that she ruined our chances to fit in.

I hated my short bangs and dorky outfits and remember a lot of shame regarding the clothes I never was able to pick out for myself. I always felt awkward and out of place. If you've ever been an oddball within the population of your peers then you know what I mean. Yet, I believed that I was a beautiful person because that is what my father always told me, every day.

I came to realize that I hated each new additional child who was born into our household because that meant I would have

119

more chores and responsibilities; changing and washing diapers since I was eight years old until I finally left home on my own at seventeen. Our house was always messy; laundry and dirty clothes to be laundered was always strewn about all over the place. My mother never did any real cleaning except on the surface such as dusting and things like that; stuffing the closets with the mess she refused or did not want to clean. I had a lot of shame and did not realize how abnormal it was living the way we lived until I got out on my own. I realized after sometime that my mother was a closet alcoholic. She would drink during the day while we were at school and my father was at work and this why she never did any cleaning. She was always verbally abusive to my father. He was a good man and never argued with her but he would slap her from time to time and this shame was a feeling that I had deep down inside.

We had a septic tank and if we would flush the toilet too many times or use too much water it would back up and it left a stench all over the house, smelling like a sewer from the basement to the very top. Even today when I smell something similar to that aroma...I just get a flashback on remembering those days at home and how embarrassing and the shame it used to bring me to bring my friends over to visit.

At the age of seventeen I got a job babysitting for my neighbor. She was a young woman, age twenty-eight, and she accepted me for what I was; a young teenager in her adolescence. I would clean her house and watch her kids every day. She talked with me and shared adult conversations. That is where I met Bradley, her stepson. I thought he was my great escape.

After six months of flirting, I lost my virginity, and became pregnant the first time that I had sex. I decided to have an abortion because I was going to be a senior the following year and it seemed to me at that time that I had no other choice. Plus my parents would have killed me had they known. But I felt I could not go to them with this burden, which was too hard for me to bear at such a young age. It was a devastating experience because deep in my heart I really wanted to have this baby, but due to the circumstances I knew it could never be. I never even told Bradley that I was pregnant which made it even worse because I had to live with this problem all by my lonesome; at the same time it was exciting to be involved in this drama that I was living.

I soon learned, but did not know at the time, Bradley was a drug addict. At this point in my life I had never used drugs other than marijuana, uppers and prescription drugs. I did not consider them to be of any harm because they did not change me but only made me feel good. I was too hungry for a relationship with the opposite sex than to have an open mind about his shortcomings. I left home at seventeen to be with Bradley, the new love of my life. I stayed with him and his family in Brooklyn; at the same time dropping out of school in my senior year. I got pregnant with my second child; a daughter named Janay.

We moved out of his mother's house and got our own apartment. He was never at home and I never asked him where he was or where he had been. I learned later that he was living to use and using to live; drugs, that is.

During my pregnancy I spent all my time with his mom who was very good to me in helping me to prepare for the birth of my baby. I remember when the baby came that Bradley got mad because the baby turned out to be a girl instead of a boy.

He continued to get loaded night and day, not caring for me or our baby. I recall saying to him: "If that stuff is so great, give me half of it." And he did; thus giving me my wings to the everlasting affliction of drug addiction and that's when I took my first hit of shooting heroin. I got sick but felt good to be alive in order to be worthy to be with him; the man I loved. I needed to do this and that was a big mistake, trying to live a life to please my man; when I should have used my common sense and lived to please myself. I began sharing his drugs with him whenever he would come home and I also shot cocaine. I never took the route of pills or snorting cocaine. I started right out as a shooter and when I did try snorting there was no comparison.

One day I came to my senses and realized that I needed to get

121

away from Bradley and his family, the drugs and the illegal ways of life. His mother and father were affiliated with the mob, running numbers and whatever else they might encounter. I didn't know and did not want to know. It was a very sick situation. Even though they were a close-knit family, they were at the same time a very dysfunctional family.

I would get phone calls and knocks on my front door with personal greetings from people on the dark side, actually monsters of sin regarding my husband, holding up people with an ice pick, and his dastardly despicable inhumane deeds even included murder. It was very wild for me; the craziness and the insanity that goes on with people and their addiction. I just could not relate to it but soon throughout the years, in my own insidious abnormal behavior, I became just as ruthless, if not worse because of my own addiction.

I called my brother Steve. He came with some of his friends and moved me out from our apartment in Brooklyn back home. I went back there to visit one day and there was no Bradley, his actions by the wages of sin had met his own feat, death. But I still kept in contact with his mother because she and I were real close friends.

Upon my arrival back at home, my father was really happy to see me again coming to my senses. I wish I could have said the same for my mother but she was not happy in the least. She said, "You made your bed, now lie in it." I knew at that moment hearing those words coming from her that I could not live at home any longer. The kitchen was too small for two women to cook in. In other words, two women cannot live in the same house and rule. So, I got my own apartment along with my new boyfriend who would visit me a couple times during the week. (A bootie call.)

I enrolled in a business college. It was a two-year course and I am happy to say that I completed it earning a degree in secretarial sciences. It was a great responsibility as well as an experience for me; giving me personal satisfaction seeing this endeavor all the way through. I was not using drugs during this time but I did drink. It was Herefords Chocolate Cow. It tasted like a chocolate milkshake and it was good. That's the thing about becoming an alcoholic, in the beginning of alcoholism you start sampling the alcohol beverages that taste sweet as you slowly become an alcoholic. I smoked pot on the weekends and I was living just a normal life or what I thought at the time was normal. I got rid of my old boyfriend and started seeing someone new. I got a secretarial job at Union Carbide in Manhattan and was feeling good about myself and my accomplishments at this point in my life, my daughter and my freedom.

I must admit it was hard getting up early in the morning; walking my daughter to the child care center in her stroller two miles from home and walking another mile to the train station to get to work. By the end of the day I was tired and whipped but I was handling it and I enjoyed my new life being single and responsible; carrying the load on my own shoulders; shopping every week; getting along with my bosses and co-workers. I was living well.

One night I went to a club and met a guy named Paul; who turned out to be an apostil of Satan. During this time I did not go out that much or socialize because of the vast responsibility I had as a single parent with a little girl and my job. My girlfriends who I worked with at the time persuaded me to take a break; come up for some air. We exchanged phone numbers and talked for quite a while. Paul came over to visit me and asked me if I wanted to indulge in some smack (heroin). I accepted while being surprised at the same time that he was into drugs. You can't judge a book by its cover. He did not strike me as the type of person who would do drugs. He had a nice car and a good job as a nurse. He was the perfect functional addict. I really fell head over heals for Paul and our romance blossomed from that winter to spring until I found out that he had another woman who was expecting his baby.

Learning of this news rally hurt me and more than that I was angry that he had not been honest with me in telling me what was going on. At this point I was in love with him but I was not satisfied with being number two.

I decided to move to California on a whim. I had met a friend of Paul's and we were communicating. I asked him what he was going to do this particular summer and he said he was going to San Francisco with his girl which sounded like a good idea to me. I asked him if he needed a roommate. He replied, "Yeah, bring your little girl and come on." So, we did.

I quit my job, sold my furniture and moved to good oh California by way of Florida with some of my friends. I have always been an impulsive, fly-by-the-night type of girl. I arrived in San Francisco with only eleven dollars in my pocket and David (my friend) and his girlfriend picked me and my daughter up at the airport. They had a nice three-bedroom apartment on Haight Street. It was one of greatest summers I ever had.

I scammed unemployment thoroughly and enjoyed everything about living in the Haight Ashbury District with its historical attraction of the birth of Love, Peace and Happiness. (Getting high.) To me it was like a dream come true; the friendliness of all the people that I would meet. The liberalism of life in San Francisco was like paradise and I understood then and there why people from all over the United States and the world would come to San Francisco to live. It was because you can do whatever you want to do and no one absolutely no one cared.

Soon, thereafter, Paul arrived. He left his woman back in New York and came to San Francisco, California, to look for and be with me which I had hoped he would. I felt very special for this act of manliness on his behalf. Drugs were not the vocal point of my life during this time, even though I did shoot up every now and then, but they soon would be now that Paul had entered into my life again.

We would indulge in smack (heroin) maybe twice a month, we were what you called chpisters, only on occasions; from twice a month it became only weekends then twice a week and from there whenever possible.

We move to the country to Sonoma, we both had decent jobs, two cars and we thought at the time it was really fly to do smack

124

and at the same time have things in place. Little did we know that we were functional addicts and only fooling ourselves because the bottom falls out of everything sooner or later when you do drugs. We were only fooling ourselves. We would get high only at home and only after Janay, our daughter, was in bed asleep. Little by little there were no onlys; our lives had become totally unmanageable. We could not afford our rent, could not buy food and everything around us was falling apart. Our disease of drug addiction was taking precedent and progressing at the rate of a malignant cancerous tumor; spreading and spreading and spreading. So, to get a grip on things we decided to make another geographical move back to New York. No matter where you go, no matter where you move, no matter where you hide, you can't hide from yourself.

At this point domestic violence was becoming a part of my life and in full cycle. I remember almost from the very start that Paul had shown this type of behavior toward me and almost anything would trigger it. This was strange to me being that I was never hit as a little girl by my father. At first I did not understand it but I figured that Paul must have really loved me to treat me this way. Later, after the damage was done, he would apologize. We had a two-way abusive relationship. I would abuse him verbally and he would abuse me physically. I guess it goes back to when I was a child and my mother would abuse my father in the same way.

Anyway, it wasn't all that bad, so I thought, because he loved me. We would reverse roles working on jobs. Paul would work graveyard, midnight to 8 a.m. until he got tired and then I would go to work. We were together for a total of fourteen years. Through our relationship I had three more children who were all born at home. We turned out to be a very close dysfunctional family. I lost all my thoughts and in the process, I let go of every interest in life except dope; losing complete sight of my own individuality that I had at that time.

As our addiction became progressively worse, so did the violence. That is one of the things that drugs can do to you; leaving you out of touch with reality. My self-esteem was low and

125

my life was hopeless. I was lazy and not attentive to my children and their needs to be healthful and strong-minded in this confused world; depending on dope to be in a good mood, depending on dope to make me happy, depending on dope to keep me alive. I blamed everyone and everything on my own shortcomings, taking no responsibility to be the head of my own life.

We spent many years moving from house to house and each time it turned out the same. We would start out all right but eventually the drugs became the center of attraction and the attention that we were trying to avoid once again; spending all our money on drugs and very little for food or the bills, for that matter. We just kept copping (buying) dope until all the money was gone and when the money ran out we would detox or at least Paul would. My habit was so bad that I would do things to get money in order to support my drug addiction. I would do all types of scams, making withdrawals from the bank with my ATM card knowing that there was no money in my account.

On all of the jobs that I had while strung out, I would steal credit cards or anything that had value to support my habit. As a matter of fact, I can't remember any job during my addiction where I did not steal. It was just a way of life for me because I was a slave to my habit of darkness within in my soul; a slave to drug addiction and I could not settle for not getting high. If there was a way to get some money I did it, hook or crook.

When my youngest son was two, I decided to leave Paul because I could not take the abuse any longer. So, I left and went to a shelter with my kids. They found me a room to live with belongings, yet my children ended up going to Child Protection Services.

I came up with this brainstorm of an idea and appealed to the court to let my children live with their father, admitting that I was a drug addict and he wasn't; it worked and the children ended up living with Paul.

While I was living in the shelter, Paul got involved with a younger woman; she was eighteen. When I got out and went back

126

home, he told me it was over. Even though I had left him, I felt betrayed and very hurt. Here was this woman living in my home, cooking in my kitchen, sleeping under my sheets with my husband and raising my kids; what a joke, a kid raising kids, was my thoughts. I had a lot of resentment as far as my feelings were but I bit the bullet and left.

At this time I changed my drug of choice (heroin) and started shooting cocaine. I also wanted recovery but I was not ready to give it up. I went hog wild, using drugs as no means to an end; living in and out of hotels and enjoying the newfound freedom that was upon me as I was no longer with Paul and no responsibilities as far as raising my kids. No man's old lady and no kids' mom. I started to feel totally worthless; feeling ashamed that I could not get my life together and reclaim my children. The whore that Paul used to call me for years became a manifestation that I started to live turning myself out at the age of thirty-five; my virtue was gone and at that time I did not care.

Being alone without any family, I began to integrate with all types of generic lives. I learned the mastering art of boosting (stealing) because prostitution, even though I did it, messed with my psyche and I never really liked it. But don't get me wrong, I was always out there turning tricks when the stores closed, when the boosting was over for the day.

I would put myself in so much grave danger as a prostitute that I was almost murdered at least twice. I shot so much cocaine, mainly in my legs, that I could not find a vein; in other words, all of my veins in my arms were burnt out from shooting drugs for so many years. With the shape that my body was in I could have made *Alien Three: The Movie*. I had so many abscesses at this time and my body was really scarred. I would not go out of my house without stockings to cover up the scars that showed the wear and tear of a drug addict. Today, I still have those scars but I don't hide them as much because I am freed from the hideous embarrassment of once being a drug addict.

One day I tried smoking crack and I enjoyed it. This, I concluded, was the solution to my problem. I no longer had to

127

worry about shooting drugs or scarring my body any more with needle marks or suffering from a lot of years of total insanity—tricking, stealing—you name it and I did it twice or better.

I was arrested numerous times, mainly for stealing and sometimes for prostitution. I was in and out of county jail for three years and finally after writing so many bad checks with one of my partners in crimes; I went to prison. That is when and where I came to grips with recovery. Prison was the break that I needed. Strange but true, as it is with so many other people who are or have been caught up in addiction; once you experience prison you either stop, continue again or die. I had a complete change of heart. I realized that I was either going to prison for a long time or I was going to die suffering in my addiction.

I found the Lord Jesus Christ in July 1994 while in The Chowchilla Prison for Women with over four thousand inmates. I worked every day on my recovery. I did everything that I possibly could to make it happen and complete. I went to AA/NA—Alcohol and Narcotics Anonymous—Bible study and anything else of a positive nature to keep me focused, thus eliminating the demon within my soul that had possessed me for so many years. I was happy for the first time in a long time of my life, more than I could remember for years.

After leaving prison, I was determined to stay clean. Now, mind you, while I was in prison I could have gotten high, as a matter of fact, two of the women who were my cellies were dealing heroin. In other words, if you wanted to get high bad enough, you can find it even behind the prison walls, guaranteed but I was determined to stay clean. I was very anxious to see my kids but they would not release me because I had a hold on me from another city but I didn't trip; I just did the three weeks that they requested along with a drug core program that they wanted me to do.

Then one day my counselor came to me and told me that she wanted me to go to a residential treatment program, which was an in-house residence for people in recovery. This request totally tripped me out. As a matter of fact, I freaked out because I could not understand why I had to go to a residential program when in fact I was doing so well with the program that I was already in.

I asked her why she was doing this to me and as I related this to her, my parole officer demanded that I go. So, I had no other choice but to abide by the court's ruling or so I thought. I tried my complete best to use all the tools that had been given to me to combat my addiction and to no avail. Three weeks later, I relapsed; cashed in my food stamps and got some crack, because I thought it was unfair. The treatment, the way they were treating me and insisting that I go to a residential treatment program.

I soon learned, or rather I already knew, that that was stinking thinking. In other words, as a drug addict sometimes we look for excuses in order to justify continuing to use drugs. When in reality, it's all an excuse.

During this period of relapse, it came to me that this was one of the worse times in my life as a drug addict and I did not enjoy it in least bit. I was part of a façade, a masquerade; cemented in my mind that this was the way out, that this was the way to cope with the stress and the pressures of everyday life that everyone must go through throughout their lives and using dope was my avenue of dealing with this.

I went on a wild binge of smoking crack. Within seven days I had sold everything that I had accumulated and worked for all behind another hit of the pipe; the glass dick, the everlasting eluding feeling of being high. This was the worst feeling I ever had being high because I had made an amends; a covenant with God while in prison not use again and now I had turned my back on him and chose to ride in the car with Satan. Damn, it made me feel lower than low. I am glad to say today that my relationship with the Lord is back at square one and I intend for it to remain that way. That's the good thing about God; he will never turn his back on you no matter how low you get, no matter how many times you make a mistake, he will forgive you but the other side of making those mistakes is payback. Yes, we all must pay back for any wrong we do or have done. It's called "Reaping what you sew." And even though I was at the epitome of emptiness He has always been a friend when there were no friends and the best part of it all is that I can call him; call him anytime day or night and you know what, He is always there and I am so happy that my Higher Power exists within him because I can do all things through Christ who strengthens me. I never want to lose the oneness that I now have with Jesus today.

Being awarded to the drug court, I had to report back every seven days and when I did not they sent out the drug patrol to find me and they always eventually did. Now, that I think about all the dramatization of being a drug addict while I was tweaking —shooting heroin, smoking crack—drinking and everything else, I realize I really did not enjoy any of it. I was really trying to fill a void by getting the last rush of being high. My drug core counselor could not believe that I was back in jail after being clean for so long while in prison.

But you see prison is only a shelter in which if you choose to be clean you can be. Once you are out on the streets, no longer bonded by society within the prison walls, no longer under the protective custody of the state, no longer under the total influence of the demonic spirit of Satan and able to do in essence what you want to do; it is then and there that the truth or consequences must be shown, it is then and only then that you have the complete control to inevitably make the right or wrong choice; to do or don't do and I risked that with many regrets.

My counselor suggested that I join The Jalani House for women, a drug rehabilitation residential program for women and I am glad that I am an ongoing in-patient resident. I agreed that I needed its program to help me. God has begun to do a good work within me today. That's the gist of my addiction.

However, I must tell you that I lived like a white tornado. A day in my life was like...maybe a month in someone else's. I would do so many things in order to support my habit but today I'm getting better and I hope that the sharing of my story will help someone else not take the road of a drug addict.

As I look back now on my life and listen to the other women in the program—who are products of child abuse, drug abuse, molestation and parental abuse, when they are in the middle of the room in the circle, sitting in that chair sharing their stories—it comes to mind that any of the above incidents can stay and breed into shame that you have about yourself within the life that you lead while growing up. I understand because I was a victim of it all. The empowering thing about it is that you really don't know until you start to live as an adult and begin to face the realities of life, but yet it seemed all exciting to me at the time even though on the dark side of the flesh there was something about boosting (stealing) that really brought out the adrenaline within me; walking down the street with a television on my shoulder or when I would go to sleep at night, even in jail, I would get the same rush in my dreams where I would dream of stealing and getting high. I believe the dreams you dream for the most part are based upon the life you live. I would dream of stealing and getting away. I know that is far from normality but that's what I dreamt; using credit cards, picking someone's pocket or just hooking up with someone who had the same thing in mind as I did (stealing) and the sad part about that is that many of those individuals I did not even know. That's the life of a drug addict; you don't have to know that person as long as you both have one common goal. They were just people off the streets living that life and if the idea sounded good, I did it. That's a big problem with people hooked on drugs; they are scandalous and they will do things, bad things, to support their habit but I would get off on doing these things more so than getting high. I can't explain it but it was exciting.

I know now what I felt was false courage, false thinking. You go out being fearless when in reality you are so afraid of being yourself that you bury yourself within yourself, embedded in your soul is the spirit of Satan; being in danger with your life; ignoring any consequences you might face; yes, even death and the sad part about it all is that you start to believe it, thinking that this is your choice and that you wanted to live a life by default.

I was such a cold hustler that I would not even lie down to go to sleep after an eight-day drug binge; that's being up all day and all night for eight days straight and, believe you me, there was no way that I felt the drugs at this stage of getting high but still in all, I kept on and on and on getting high until I just burnt myself out and fell asleep. Wherever I was, whether on the sidewalk, in the hallway or anywhere, I would crash, until I got so crazy that I had to get arrested. They had to arrest me because I was out of mind, out there for so long and this was the only way for me to come down at this stage of insanity in my life. Now, that's insane. I'm sure you would agree.

I did not like being alone by myself. I found it to be very hard but I loved the freedom of no responsibility. Today I love the quality time that I can give myself; an hour of reading, a moment for prayer and time for meditation and being with my Higher Power; God, which is a miracle for me today that I can attest to. As I look back now, I can remember the terrible feeling of tweaking all night and watching the sun come up. What a horrible feeling; walking those streets four years in a row after getting out of prison and watching the Christmas lights, never calling my kids. When I would go to jail, I would come down and feel oh so ashamed with the life that I was leading that when I would get out of jail, I could not deal with the notion of thinking about the hurt and pain, and the misery and the suffering, that I was taking myself through; possessed by the spirit of the demon, so much so that as soon as I would get out of jail, I would go straight to the drug dealer and buy drugs to numb the pain and the reality of seeing things as they truly were.

If someone were to ask me at that time what was I doing, I would not have had an answer. I did not know. I remember selling diapers or stealing diapers for my baby. I would not even bring the diapers back home to my own child, my own baby, because I was too busy supporting my drug habit, smoking crack, as much as I possibly could, my disease was cunning and so baffling, just like Satan, light years away.

Today I am learning to forgive myself for the transgressions that I have done to my children as well as myself and I know that I am now doing the right thing to make my life whole again and it's not ever going to be easy. I am a grateful person today, very grateful about the smallest things that one may normally take for granted; taking baby steps, one at a time. I love it when I sweat and I love it when I hurt. It sounds crazy and I'm not masochistic but it lets me know that in order to get well, completely well, I have to feel what I feel when I feel it; to let the release of the pressure go however it must be released, even if it's puking it out like when were are sharing stories about our addiction and those feelings start to come forth from our sharing.

I can feel it when my fourteen-year-old daughter decided to go and live with her grandmother because I could not give her the love she so desperately needed and rightfully deserved. I remember giving her permission to do so because I understood her dilemma at that particular time and there was nothing for her to come to, that terrible feeling of failure, the love I showed to my daughter was there and I said, "Yes." It was very hard to live with and I could taste the bitterness of it in my mouth. And I had to leave the group session to be alone with my feelings. Even though it was full of sadness, I swallowed it to suppress it, yet it was still mine.

That night I was still thankful to feel that feeling and grateful to know that all my feelings were wrapped up in me somewhere that I can reach out and grasp that feeling again. As long as I can sit through those sessions and embrace those feelings again, I know that I am only human but it makes me feel good. I know the life I lead may have contributed, rather has been a factor, in my daughter choosing the life she now leads.

She's now twenty-one and married and I was told that she was raped, even though I don't believe it's true, then again I don't really know. I was also told she is doing cocaine, and my heart just aches for her, along with being with a man that abuses her and I just hurt for her. I'm terrified that she is in danger with her life and I know that all I can do to stay strong for her is to be here in recovery and be here for her in case she needs me. There is nothing else I can do but that and pray to God that she will be all right. Worrying is sin and it will not help and I have to constantly renew my faith in my mind, knowing that God is going

133

to watch over her and take care of my baby.

I am grateful for my other children, who are ten, thirteen and fourteen, living with their father, Paul. I hope someday to have them reunited with me. If it's God will. I want to have a positive impact on their life. Paul is married again, very hooked on his addiction to heroin, living to use and using to live and about to fall flat on his face. I am so glad that I am in recovery. It has been five years and knowing that I am here for my children and it scares me because I love them with all my heart as well as myself and it is so much more today than it ever has been.

I don't have a big ego but my self-esteem and the gift of appreciating who you are is so blissful. They now have hope when they come and visit me and it is so enlightening for us all. At the same time I can see a lot of emotional scars that only time can heal from living a very dysfunctional life as children in a drug-infested home and they are real needy and I am grateful that they saw me here at this program that when they left they carried in their heart some hope knowing at the same time that their father is still using. It is sad but it's true and my daughter being sexually molested by her stepbrother. I just pray that they will be all right. It's funny, or rather it is strange, how life is so insane when you are on drugs; especially when you deny everything that is true.

I often ask myself how I could have ever left them knowing that their father was a drug addict too. I know life is going to be hard but I am committed to my recovery program because that's the only way I can ever be there for my children and more importantly for myself because if I don't have me, I have nothing.

Today I am hungry for information; being in a safe and clean environment where I can cry and talk with my sisters about everything regarding the monsters that have been chasing me all these years. I do understand more about the paradoxes of recovery, of being spiritual; period with the Lord. What used to save me out there in the world will kill me now. I am striving for a very strong foundation because my life is my own responsibility and I realize no one owes me anything.

I am strong in the Lord today. I read the word of God every

day just like I needed the fix every day, and I am willing to put in my recovery the same that I put into my addiction. That is the attitude that I have and will have as long as I put Christ Jesus first in my life, as he will be from now on as long as I live.

I am seeking his knowledge and grace through prayer and understanding, being overwhelmed with his mercy and grace. I try to take each and every moment to make it positive even if it is a bad thing that is happening to me; learning to try and grow and appreciate them and praise the Lord for everything negative and positive. I will be 40 years old in December and that's when life is supposed to start, or at least that is what I am told. So I am right on time. I've got the tools and I know, and I know, and I know that I can make it this time, my faith and will are strong through Jesus Christ who strengthens and keeps me.

BOTTOM LINE

A CRACKHEAD IS A JUNKIE, A diseased sickness of the mind that will never be conquered. A disease sickness that you choose by choice to live in. If you think you can then you're only fooling yourself. If you think you can then you're only fooling yourself. And if you do think that you can, you will never be happy or content with the life that you lead. The only way you can have complete freedom from this infectious disease of drug addiction is to give your life to Christ and let God become your center of attention for living; or as some people have suggested, your Higher Power. Whatever it may be and whatever it takes, you need to address it and suffer your habit. That's right, suffer your habit. How does one suffer their habit? Easier said than done. The only way to suffer your habit is to give it up and in doing so you will suffer. You will suffer the lust of your flesh. You will suffer so hard and so deep that you might feel like dying but don't die yet. Because as you suffer each day, each moment, each waking hour, you will begin to conquer your addiction. If you keep your hand on the plow and don't look back, you will prevail.

The bottom line is this: if you stay hooked on crack, you are

136

selling your soul to Satan for the rock. There's another rock that you don't have to burn on the screen. There is another rock that will not keep your mind in a whirlwind, never knowing up from down, never knowing your left from your right. There is another rock that costs you nothing; that rock is The Rock of Ages. The rock whose substance is not made up of man, whose substance is not diluted with shame, guilt and agony; the rock that can never be shattered into pieces. The rock that can hold you through the trials and tribulations, through the good and the bad and that rock is Jesus.

The finale of all of this for the one who is strung out on crack is simple, hard and sincere. I am putting this in the bluntness of terms to the lowest degree of understanding that I can think of and that is this: if you stay strung out on crack cocaine or any other drug, the life that you know will either come to an end by being homeless, in prison or death. Sooner that you allotted God-given time to be here on earth and if you are fortunate enough to cheat being homeless or in jail, misery and death most assuredly without a doubt will be the end of your doom.

Now, if this is not enough for you to want to quit, then go on and rest in peace, in the penalty of your sin as you give your soul to Lucifer, as you wait on that judgment day to burn in hell. It's your choice. That's the beauty of it all; you have the choice. Pay now or pay later but one thing is for sure: you will pay for each and every deed and act that you do as a drug addict. But the good part of it is this: you have a chance if you let Christ in your life. Jesus said, "Behold I stand at the door and knock. If anyone will let me in, I will come in and sup with him or her." He is saying this: I will be your bridge over the trouble water. I will be your light at the end of the tunnel. I will your bread when you are hungry. I will be you drink when you are thirsty. I will be your all and all.

Hey! You tried everything, why not try Jesus? Is it really worth it to sell your soul? No, but the answer is within you. If I can quit along with the other people between these pages, so can you too. All it takes is a made-up mind. So, ask God or the Higher Power in which you identify as God, but let's be real, there's only One God, One Faith and One Baptism, and the only way to get to God is through Jesus his son. For Jesus said, "I am the way, the truth and the life no man cometh unto the Father except by me." Just do it and take it one day at a time. If nothing else you will stop investing in the bottomless pit that is sucking you dry. Just think how much money you have lost smoking crack. I know for myself that during my addiction I could have at least three houses and all the amenities that one could hope for if I were not strung out on crack. How much money have you lost? Never mind, you probably cannot even calculate it all and that should give you even more of an incentive to quit.

Now, I can walk around, have a hundred dollars in my pocket, and still have eighty dollars by the end of the week. I can walk around with five dollars and still have five dollars at the end of the day. I could not have done this by myself. I could not have come out of my addiction if it were not for God.

But the bottom line is on you.

DAVE

MY CHILDHOOD WAS PRETTY UNIQUE, somewhat quite different from the rest of my neighbors. I grew up in the state of Louisiana. We had a very strict mother and father. I thought my father was crazy and abusive because he always stayed full of that alcohol and he taught us to "Do as you are told and not as you see me do." That was his motto. My mother and father never used or abused drugs with the exception of my father; he used alcohol which is itself a drug. My family consisted of seven girls and four boys. The older kids were treated with more strictness and discipline than the younger ones who got a little bit more slack.

I had more freedom and was able to do some things I wanted to do and what I desired versus the other children. Whatever I asked my father for, as far as money and going out, he always gave it to me. My growing up as a child was half and half; most of the time I was unhappy because of the meanness of my father. We were limited with the sense of freedom that other children had but most of the time I was able to do what I wanted to do, go out and party and meet different girls; go to different places meeting people.

I never got involved with drugs during this time in my life. I remember the first time I drank beer. My dad had a little outhouse where he stashed his beer and alcohol. He had lots of beer, stacks of beer, cartons of beer, crates of beer; beer. I was about nine years old and me and my younger brother broke into that beer house and we drank two cans of beer. It made me sick because it was hot and that turned me off from drinking beer, along with the fact of seeing my father intoxicated and how it affected him. I recall my father's definition of drug use, he hated it. He always taught me and my brothers and sisters against drugs or so he thought. He always talked about it but he never actually taught us about it. He never did drugs and he knew that people who did, according to his philosophy, turned out to be nothing in life and they all ended up dead somewhere. Which was what happened to me later on; not literally but mentally, spiritually and emotionally.

Now, by hearing all about drugs throughout my childhood—watching the news and the deaths and the murders of people who were affiliated with drugs and its use and how people changed while under its influence and its effect, how they acted—just really turned me off against the thought of using drugs and I know now that is why I did not get into it at an early age. I wish I had not at all. However, that would never be.

We moved to Stockton, California, and one day at lunchtime, while I was in high school, one of my friends, a teammate on the football team (by the way, I could have gone to college on a football scholarship. I had all the tools to be a running back in the NFL. I will never know about that one episode of what I could have been back then.), offered me some marijuana. He would be smoking marijuana every day at lunch. He would ask, "Hey, man, you wanna hit this joint? You wanna hit this joint?" And I would always tell him, "No, no, man, I don't want none of that." Then one day he called me a daredevil and that was a challenge. Don't dare me because I must might want to take you up on it, maybe. And that is what I did. I took the dare. I hit the joint and said, "See, man, this stuff didn't do anything to me, here take it back."

So the next day he offers me to hit the joint again. "Dave, you wanna hit this joint?" I said, "Why not, it didn't do nothing to me the first time." But this time I felt it and so I hit it again; then I said to him, "Do you have any more of that pot?" On the third day and then on the fourth day and again on the fifth day, it was on. Until this day I am sorry that I ever smoked pot because it became the avenue that led me from one drug to another. I began to spend a lot of money on pot and I began to sense: "Wow, what's happening here?" because my thinking started changing and I knew that this was not rational. Everywhere I went—to parties, dances—I had to have my weed, my pot, in order to have good time.

Oh, I really did like the high. It really didn't do anything to me at the time; at least this is what I thought except that it made me real mellow, gave me the giggles and for me that was good because I was kind of a quiet person. Smoking pot let me open up to my true feelings. I was really partying all the time; me and my cousin.

I remember going over to one of my sisters' houses one night; she lived in San Francisco about ninety miles north from Stockton. Her husband was passing around the coke plate around (cocaine). He asked if me or my cousin had ever snorted cocaine.

I said, "Yeah." Knowing that I never had and my cousin gave me that look because he also knew I had never snorted cocaine before. So, I took the plate and snorted cocaine for the very first time in my life while sipping on a couple of beers. Then I smoked some coke in a cigarette. Man, I felt good. I was really mellow, really mellow. Now, it's about time to go and I get up and reach for the doorknob and I fell right on my butt in slow motion and everyone started teasing me but I never forgot that night; the rush, the high of cocaine and its feeling of euphoria and saying to myself that drugs can be something else.

I didn't get involved in coke too soon after that but I did like the way it made me feel. The draining effect running through my body made me feel like I never felt before and the idea of doing the ever-so-popular elite drug, coke, was something that would stay with me for a long time. It started to make me spend my money just like when I was buying weed except it cost more; twenty-five dollars for a quarter gram of powered cocaine.

Buying this drug while going out and partying, my sex life was good, I had the talk, a rap like no other, a sharp car; making money every day, working on Nob Hill parking cars in the exclusive area of San Francisco, the cash was flowing in and the supply for my drugs…man, it was on. OOOOOH what a rush. Man, I had the girls; they liked it and I liked it and we did what we wanted to together. Hey, what ya say? It was all good.

Then I begin focusing on my life and the roller coaster ride I was on and I told myself, "Wow, man, you really ain't yourself, going overboard with this cocaine thing." And when that thought crossed my mind, the deeper involved I became. I was in denial and yet now knowing what I truly was becoming or had become an addict; a drug addict. I never thought for one moment or even realized that it would get like this in my life but since I had never reached any disastrous points in my life which was already in the danger zone of addiction which I could not see. I didn't trip that hard on it, except for going out trying to find some more. Now, that was a disaster in and of itself, what a joke, not being able to see it.

My cocaine habit was getting totally out of hand, snorting all the time. I started spending a little too much money keeping up with my supply of supporting my habit. It's funny how something could be going on right in front of your face and you do not even realize what is exactly happening to you. They syndrome of snorting coke was getting out of hand. I had the money; so there was no problem with getting it when I wanted it but it became bizarre; out of hand, out of control; not caring what extremes I had to go through in order to satisfy my cravings, my need, my addiction.

As the years went on, how many, I can't recall; when you are an addict time means nothing to you. Time is just a void to fill in the space to continue to get high again. Time is nothing that you treasure. Time is nothing that really matters to you. Time becomes an endless, ceaseless journey of pain. Time becomes the stop sign of misery. Time becomes the time when you get your next hit, when your next paycheck comes, when the next hustle arrives; that is all that time meant to me. Time was something that in essence was dead to me.

I was still snorting cocaine throughout the years when I learned that you could rock cocaine and smoke it; crack. I kept hearing about rock cocaine and how widespread its use was in the hood of drug addiction. Yeah, I heard a lot of talk about rock cocaine but still had never tried it until one day.

I had to go to Stockton to pick up my younger brother because he was having some trouble with some of the people who lived there. So, I went to get him to come and live in San Francisco. I knew this woman who was a bus driver who had a big house with lots of rooms upstairs and downstairs. I set him up with a room and he moved in downstairs the first night and the second night I went to visit him he was living upstairs with her in her bedroom; in one night he moved from downstairs to upstairs.

After a while, I would say, a couple of months passed by and before too long, I noticed a change in him; his behavior; something out of the ordinary; something very different; just doing strange things but it was definitely a change. I would come to know that change oh so dreadfully. He would come by house late at night and ask to borrow money. While me and my family were resting peacefully there he was at two, three sometimes four o'clock in the morning asking for money. I could not understand this at the time. I would ask myself: "What is he doing up this late asking for money and why couldn't he wait until tomorrow?"

This went on for a while, then one day he and his lady friend came by my house and she introduced me and my cousin to the rock; crack cocaine.

At first when I smoked it, I didn't feel a thing just like when I first smoked pot; I didn't feel nothing. A few weeks later I, along with my cousin, went to her house where she turned us on to it again; crack that is, and again I felt nothing. I hit it (smoking from the pipe) and inhaled it and held it in my lungs—still nothing. My resistance was strong. The same resistance that's sustaining me from going back to that disintegrating road of drug addiction.

Now, the daredevil in me kept coming back for more and then it happened; I felt it. A rush, a high like I had never known in my life. Better than smoking weed or snorting cocaine simultaneously. Wow, wow, wow. The very next day I got paid from my job and I went straight over to this lady's house who had turned me on and spent three quarters of my check on the rock (crack) and as I was doing this, I thought: *I'm overspending and it takes a lot of money for this drug called crack.* I was addicted at that moment after the third time of trying it and I didn't even know it. The drug, the sensation, the feeling did something to me I had never gone through or experienced in my life of getting high, that no other drug had ever done before.

That night my whole world changed, my being would never be the same again, little did I know. I knew this was abnormal but yet and still every time I got paid I went straight over to the dealer's house to get some of that crack, that crack cocaine. The rude awakening was upon me and the beast had come to life, the monster; the crack monster.

While trying to keep my drug use a secret only to myself as far as my spending; I stopped going to the lady's house to buy my dope and started buying on the streets. I'd go and get some powder cocaine and try to cook it myself. Soon, thereafter, I ran into a connection; a drug dealer that I had no problem with at all to buy my drugs. He was my father-in-law; an ex-player, pimp, the original O-G (old gangster.) He told me, "As long as you are spending your money, you might as well spend it with me and get it properly served to you the way it should be." And I did. He gave me my money's worth and even more making sure I would get strung out. I spent a lot of money with him and he even extended my credit line. I was getting deeper and deeper in debt supporting my habit of smoking crack.

Man, I just didn't realize or couldn't believe what was

144

happening to me but I was steady, doing it day and night; smoking crack cocaine. I started staying out all night spending all my money; walking the streets in dangerous territories, in the projects from house to house; around scandalous people, searching for the crack, searching for the rock, searching for the elusive high that could never be contained no matter how much I smoked or how much I did, but by me being bold I just never really was afraid of the danger and the darkness of my soul in which I was walking in. I had become a walking zombie; a character of the living dead.

Then it started getting scarier. I began to get involved with the dirt and the people who dwelled in it; crackheads, dirty people, other addicts. They did all kinds of things in order to get high and me on the scene being green and new to the game of addiction just didn't know. I was generous with my dope and shared it. This is when my addiction started getting the best of me. I lost a lot of money being nice and sharing because I was not using that much. Splurging with other addicts was devastating to my finance.

While staying out all kind of hours of the night it began to affect my family life; my wife and my children. She would say, "Whatever you are doing do it at home." She had no idea what she was asking me to do. So, I brought my drug use into my home and that was a bad mistake because she wanted to try it and one night when her father was at our house, she asked me for some and I told her: "No, I'm not giving you anything. It's on the table if you want to do it, you get it." And she did.

I soon learned that the few people I trusted to cook my dope for me, because I did not know how, were holding back keeping a lot for themselves; flakes that rested on the sides and the bottom in the glass of the cooker bottle. I remember saying, "Why those lowdown dirty dogs." Beating me on the cooks; the amount that I was supposed to get. So I learned to cook it and I cooked it good. My addiction was getting deeper and deeper into darkness. Hey, "Slipping Into Darkness." WAR...I began missing work and my attendance was becoming very sloppy. I started staying up all night after getting paid on payday every week and

145

wake up the next morning and would not go to work after smoking that stuff all night. I just couldn't, not after having no sleep, none; absolutely none. I wanted to in my mind but I was too tired. I had no energy; up all night smoking crack. It just seemed to me that there was never enough.

The more I smoked crack the more I wanted to smoke it. Disbelief set in of what I was doing to myself and what I had become but I still did it. Crying out for help to find a way out of this dilemma did not come easy. My cousin would try and talk to me and try to slow me down but it didn't do any good. It was on and I was on a roll, full scale, like a mad rabid dog.

At this point it's hard for me to keep pressing on with this story because I really would like to forget about it. From time to time I reflect on just some of things I did and it's enough to keep me going straight in my recovery but anyway I'm going to try to continue the best I can. It's real hard, man, but at this time in my life this was a totally addicted me.

Yeah, I began to more or less run the streets on the corners, copping (buying) my own dope; having a pocket full of money amongst the scum and the trash which was a danger in and of itself. Very dangerous; jeopardizing my life of getting beat down for my money or my dope but I did it anyway; searching for crack. Control was dismantled within me and my life was out-to-lunch when it came to getting some more rock, some more crack to get high. All this right in front of my face, screaming at me, wow, but I just didn't have the will powder to take back control of my life and quit right away and I knew my addiction had the best of me completely. I had become an angel of darkness obsessed with the demonic spirit of Satan. I wanted to quit; yet at the same time I didn't want to quit. The high was too good, real good; so good that I just could not give it up.

While getting high, I must admit, at times it wasn't all that bad. I had a lot of good times, or so I thought. Going out staying high; having females in the same click, same environment oftentimes, it was a big freak show, an orgy. Actually, smoking the rock sometimes can be a party until it's all gone and your high starts to come down and the party is over and reality sets in and you don't have any more. Whew, what a trip. That's the thing about smoking crack, when the last little bit is gone and you want more you; you start to wonder how to get some more after spending all your money. I mean all your money, your whole check, you still want more. That was the worst feeling about getting high that I ever felt during my addiction to want to get high and can't unless you do something wrong, very wrong; SIN.

I started borrowing money; something that I never would do but I had to have my regular daily high. My addiction was costing me two to three hundred dollars a day and I had to have it. It's really bad at this point, really bad and it even gets worse.

I began to steal and I never stole before in my life. I had no need to steal but my diseased addicted mind, bound by the forces of evil, started stealing. It hurt me so bad to be the person that I had become but my heart was convicted to support my habit. It was so easy to do. I would go into a store and walk right out with whatever I wanted. No problem, and I would turn around and trade what I stole for drugs. My biggest thing was taking alcohol off the supermarket shelves. I was bootlegging alcohol; hey; it was all good. I could take up to four fifths at one time, five to six times a day at the same stores, walk out like it was the thing to do; unseen, untouched. I was breaking them off real strong and I got good. I got real good at it but you are never too good to do wrong and not get caught; and that's what started happening to me. I began to get caught and I would end up in jail on petty theft charges and as soon as I got of jail I would do it again, and again and I got caught again and again and had to go to jail but I had to have my high.

Sometimes I sold drugs and ended up smoking up my profit. So, I never made nothing. I got put out at home, rather I left running the streets to maintain my high. I had too much pride to ask my brothers or sisters for shelter; so I would end up walking the streets two to three nights in a row; staying high all night, walking the streets. I became a homeless person. I would get my welfare check and as soon as I got it I would spend it all getting

147

high on crack and would not even keep myself a room. Now that's sad, ain't it? Real sad, but that's all that mattered to me; getting high on crack. Ain't that about nothing but anyway it was all good back then.

I slept in abandon cars. I could get no one to take me in. When people find out that you are a drug addict, nobody wants to have anything to do with you. In a sense you can't blame them because some of those same people got burnt by me because I would steal or borrow money from them and never pay them back. I spent many a cold night wanting to lie down and get some sleep. I had no shelter. So, I would ride the buses all night just for warmth and some kind of comfort away from the elements; ride the bus and stay up all night. Man, that was cold; a very cold feeling to be walking around the streets at four or five o'clock in the morning and not have a place to say. This was my worst experience as a drug addict smoking crack; sleeping in cars and on the streets. Sometimes I would go a whole week and even longer without taking a bath. All I used to do was wash my face and move on. I smelt like garbage. I lived in a shack of Jamestown Street; a drug house, a crack house, a place to get high.

There were so many evil spirits in that house; I cannot begin to tell you. Me and cousins would fight almost every night like dogs over dope; getting high and wanting to get high even more. Police would chase the dealers off the street and I would let them in the house to hide in exchange for some crack so that I could continue getting my high. It was a bad thing to live like that but I did.

Three o'clock in the morning, the dope is gone and I did not want to accept that fact. So, I would go out at three or four in the morning hustling to keep getting high; stealing from the local 7-eleven or take the bus ten miles out to the nearest supermarket to steal some merchandise keeping my high on. When it seemed like the whole world was sleeping, I was the only one out on the streets looking for something to steal to continue my mission of staying high. I was a walking nightmare; a vampire possessed by the darkness of night seeking for blood.

148

I can recall this one instance when I was sleeping in this car for about three weeks or longer; a nice big Lincoln Continental. I would get high and crawl back in it and fall asleep, yeah, yeah, yeah. This one particular night, it was raining real hard, a storm. I got in the car; started getting high and there was this cat that would always crawl under the car for shelter, but this one night he started howling along with some of his cat buddies and it was so strange and very bizarre. It started howling and meowing and growling so loud that it became eerie. It was as if he was talking to me. It stopped sounding like a cat. It became a voice speaking to me; a message, someone trying to reach me. It was real scary. Upon learning about tweaking and crack; now I know that it was Satan himself.

It's getting to be real, real sad. As for me being homeless, it was dreadful; a feeling that I cannot describe. Now, you have got to understand I was aware why I was homeless and just as well being in this predicament because there's a difference with individuals who are homeless—some don't care and some do—and I really did, deep in my heart, I really did but I could not find the control over my drug addiction to crack and the elements of its attraction; therefore, I remained weak, letting crack control me, my every waking hour, my whole being, my reason for living was to use and continue to use.

During my addiction I did some things that I totally regret and I cannot change those things as much as I would like to but I can't; what's done is done. Although regrets are in the midst, all I can do is move forward. I would go to jail all the time on those petty theft charges. Every time I got released, I would just go out and do the same thing again. I stole thousands of dollars worth of merchandise while I was stuck on stupid. I would break them off, meaning I stole all the time, get caught, go to jail and do it again. Whenever I got busted, I would humble myself while being locked down. As soon as I was released, humbleness was put on the back burner and nothing else mattered. My life continued as I was living; get high, go to jail; get out, go to jail and on and on and on.

I can recall this one particular incident. Me and a my dope fiend friend went out of town, down to San Mateo, that's twenty miles south of San Francisco, in middle of the night, in order to steal some merchandise to get some dope. We went to this store and I went in and stole four fifths of alcohol, went back in and stole four more and I said: "This is real good tonight" and I went in to get four more and I got busted; ran outside; looked around and saw that the dude who had given me a ride to the store left me and I knew that the police would be coming and I had a petty theft warrant out on me at the time and I remembered the DA telling me that if I get busted one more time for petty theft that I would go to the penitentiary.

So, here I am, in the midnight hour, in the white folks part of town and I knew I could not walk the streets; a black man that late at night. Questions would have to be answered. The buses had stopped running and I knew the police were en route. So, I found some real tall hedges and bushes; crawled in and lay there on the ground all that night; seeing rats, hearing crickets, being bit by mosquitoes and other bugs and spiders, but I told myself: "You did the crime and if you want to stay free from the jailhouse you got to ride this out," suffering the consequences and I did until six o'clock the next morning when the buses started running again, when night had finally become day once again. What a trip.

Once I was on a binge, a serious episode of smoking crack and getting high, and I wanted some more and did not have any means of getting any more. I was at my mother's house and I began to look around for some type of merchandise worth money that I could trade for some more crack. Man, I felt so bad about what I was thinking about doing. My mother was away from home visiting my sister in South San Francisco, helping her with her newborn daughter who was born premature. So, here I am coming down and that's the worst feeling you can have as an addict; coming down and wanting some more, you are aching for it, craving for it and you got to get it some kind of way, you got to have it. I started looking around my mother's house and seeing what I could trade for some more dope even though I had just gotten paid. I did not have any more money, smoking it all up, my whole check, but I still had to have some more crack by whatever circumstances I could get it and that's the thing about crack you want more and more and more and there's never enough.

Now, when I did live at my own place, I would take stuff and sell it but I never would break into other people's homes; burglary wasn't my thing. I was living with mom in Fairfield at the time and I was the only one home and I needed some more dope to keep my high going. So, I took, rather I stole, my mother's grandfather clock and her fur coat and traded them both for dope. I knew it was wrong but I had to get high, I just had to. I sold the clock and the coat with a promise to the dude who bought them that I would return to buy them back before my mother came back home. Every time I got the money to buy it back, I would go out and buy more crack. I came up with this concoction of a story to tell my mother that someone broke into her house and stole her stuff but I felt so bad and so convicted about the sin that I had committed against my mother; so I just told her the truth.

At this time I am starting to feel very suicidal because my mother loves me so much and throughout all of my addiction she stood by me when everyone else turned their back on me. She was always there; no matter what the situation; she was there giving me something to learn on, the word of God, thoughts of encouragement, food and shelter; regardless of what my condition was, mom was always mom. I felt like a dog about what I had done to her, a real dog.

I cried and I cried; until I just couldn't cry anymore. That was a traumatic chapter and time in my life that I truly hate to relive but I got to tell you this, people, so that you will know if you do get strung out you will reach the point of no return and when you reach that point there is no turning back except through God. All of this and I still was not ready to surrender yet. Even though it touched me, it hurt me deeply. It was like no other hurt in world but I was an addicted crackhead under the influence and I dared not to help myself; I just couldn't.

One Christmas, while I was living in Fairfield, I went out and stole a whole lot of toys and gifts for my kids and in the interim I stole a few goodies for myself that I could use to trade for dope and why did I do that? I ended up trading everything that I had stolen for my kids' Christmas for crack. I felt like a damn fool but I couldn't help myself. I would ask myself, "Why?" Time after time and there was never an answer. I did manage to go back out on Christmas Eve and steal some more stuff for my kids; gave them some money that had been given to me as a gift and so it wasn't all that bad for them.

I'll never forget during my addiction when I would go out and get rat packed jumped on by three or four and sometimes even more guys than that, who were drug dealers because I did not want to buy their dope, or because I was short on my money, or because I would try and pretend to buy dope and switch it, and sometimes just because they wanted to because I was a dope fiend, a crackhead, a user and they just wanted to physically abuse and hurt me. Not only me but this happened to a lot of other people strung out on crack and through all of that it still was not enough to make me quit. I would say to myself, "Well, I lived." And kept on rolling. This went on for two to three years and it's getting worse and worse. Small-town boy like me should have stayed home, should have never hit the first joint, should have never taken the first hit of crack, should have never taken the first sip of alcohol; small-town boy like me.

I can recall going to a church, the Lord's House and speaking with a preacher, a pastor, and telling him that I was hungry and that I needed food. He gave me fifty dollars; I thought here I am defrauding God's chosen one. I knew that I would have to pay for that deed but at that time it did not matter. The only thing that mattered was getting some crack. So, I thought I would just have to accept whatever punishment God wanted to give to me and pay for it later because you always have to reap what you sew. No matter what you do, good or bad, you will reap it sooner or later.

I remember another time I went to a church and talked with the pastor for a long time about God and the Bible and we really hit it off; speaking good about God and his goodness. I had an ulterior motive, however, just like the angel of light who transformed himself into the spirit of darkness. My motive at that time was all a big con; a big con in the name of crack cocaine. He too gave me fifty dollars. I felt real bad about what I had done but I had to continue supporting my habit getting high, at the same time I was praying to God not to strike me down and he didn't. This con game went on for quite a while going strong as I would talk to other Christian people and almost every one of them would give me some kind of money and I would buy more dope.

I knew in the back of my mind that one day I would have to answer for this and I did and sometimes I still do but that's just the way it is. But I've got to tell you, when you reap it's ten times as worse coming back at you. Man, that was insane. To do things like that knowing the consequence of payback. I would walk the streets sometimes with my sons and tell people that I didn't have any money and I wanted to do something nice for my sons, buy them a gift or something of that nature and each time people would reach out and give me money to help me and my boys and I would use that money to buy crack. That really hurt me to use my kids as a front to support my habit; involving my children in my drug addiction.

One night at home my wife was at work. I would let drug dealers come by my house and cut up their dope in order to get some. Well, on this one occasion while this was happening, my wife came home, got so pissed off and left. A little while later my cousin came by with another guy who wanted to cut up his dope and he left me some. I smoked so much crack that night that I started trembling. I began to start tweaking. I was so afraid, paranoid, totally frightened. I was thinking about my mother and began to cry crocodile tears and within my heart and soul I started to talk to her, telling her, "Mama, I'm so high, I don't know what to do. I'm tweaking and I am scared to death. Mama,

153

I'm so afraid. Mama, if only you were here to hold me. Mama, I'm so tired of this life. Mama, please help me. Mama, Mama. Oh, I love you, Mama. Mama, Mama. Please...PLEASE. Where's my mama? Mama, I don't know what to do. Mama, MAMA, MAMA."

That night after everyone left, I smoked so much crack I did not even want anymore. Now, believe you me, that's higher than high; that is insane. Lying there on the couch in this big empty house. The weather was real bad that night. The wind was whistling, whipping, cutting and blowing through the chimney, howling like the death of night. I could hear voices whispering real low and talking. I knew I heard these voices. I know now that it was the devil and his disciples working on me through its demonic spirit trying to conquer my soul.

I told myself, "Man, you're tweaking, you're tripping" and I began to come down but I still heard the voices; studying my spirit of possession, capturing my mind like a fish on a hook, reaching out trying to grasp my soul or maybe it was just the wind churning through the empty spaces of that house but to me it was not. I knew that it was not the wind. The voice, an unknown presence, trying to converse with me, talk to me, coming inside of me trying to run me out of the house. I thought it was the Lord talking to me, but God doesn't mix with evil spirits, right? I came all the way down that night wanting to get up and run. I kid you not, run right out the front door. Run as fast as I possibly could. Run and keep running until I could not run anymore. That's how afraid I was because Satan was right in front of me; his spirit. Have you ever seen Satan?

I did not run, I could not run. I was tweaking or so I thought that I had to stay right where I was at. Later after coming down, I gathered my senses, relaxed and told myself that whatever comes my way that we are just going to have to handle it. Yes, I said "we." But I did not know who would be handling the situation with me, but the we I was speaking of included the might and the most powerful spirit on earth and in heaven; God. I stayed there and rested until I came back to my right state of mind. That's what crack can do to you; take your mind, causing you to think all type of abnormal thoughts. Then I remembered something that happened to me earlier that day, what my wife had said to me; that she knew an old lady who was psychic and that if she wanted me out of the house and out of her life, she could make it happen. I thought for a minute that this was happening but then again what was happening to me that night was deeper than a psychic phenomena or voodoo put together. I will never forget that night in my life, never, when the spirit of God and Satan were battling for my soul.

Sometimes I would get high in front of my little children as they lay there in their crib asleep. I felt perturbed. Even though they did not know what I was doing, the depth of my soul was darkened as I thought about my addiction to crack.

Well, here comes the good part and it's about damn time after twelve years of misery and pain; twelve years of being held as a slave in bondage through my addiction, twelve years of trouble after trouble, confusion, sadness, depression, oppression; just a desolated soul existing for crack.

What made me finally surrender my addiction? I was back at home and me and the old lady are at each other arguing and just about ready to fight. She called the police on me and that's a no-no. I have never acknowledged the police being called into a family matter, never. Anyway, by the time they got there, my high was coming down and I was pretty calm and she was drunk asking them to kick me out of the house. They said they could not do that because I hadn't done anything of criminal intent.

They asked me to take a walk and I did. I started thinking about quitting. Understand this, I would quit time after time and relapse and start again, falling right back in the same trap destroying my family and my relationship with my wife and children. This went on for about three years, me trying to quit but this time I really and sincerely wanted to quit and I made up my mind that this is what I was going to do.

I learned of a rehabilitation house, a Christian program. My brother was there and he was clean, so I said why not give it a try.

I stayed there longer than my allotted time (six months) because I wanted to be strong when I came back in the world and I did not want to use again. I have now been clean for five years and I still get the craves now and then but I refuse to give in because this time I've got Jesus Christ on my side. I resist the temptation of Satan and the feeling of intolerability to cope with the dark side of my mind soon subsides.

It's getting easier these days because every day I get stronger and stronger, and I pray to God to never let me be the human being (the monster) that I once was during my addiction.

My message to those who are still using is this: you can make it if you try, but you've got to put forth some effort and then you've got to put forth some more effort and some more and some more and some more. But all it takes at the beginning is one day at a time.

And to all you drug dealers, and I am happy to say this, you will never get another dime from me. All of you need to go and get a job.

TWEAKING

WHAT IS TWEAKING? IF YOU HAVE never been around people who smoke crack or crank (methamphetamine), which is also related with tweaking, then this term means nothing to you. People who are addicted to crack often use this term when someone is doing something that can be considered abnormal behavior.

For example, one might say that a person is tweaking when he or she just sits, or stands still in a certain place for a period of time; suspended in animation. One might say in the drug world that a person is tweaking when he or she talks a lot, or to the other extreme is just quiet. One might say in the drug world of crack that a person is tweaking when he or she sits in a state of paranoia from smoking crack; thinking that someone is chasing them, thinking that someone is about come through the door, thinking that the bark of a dog outside is coming after them, thinking that someone is looking at them from the house across the street with its lights on, thinking that someone is following them and that the police are about to break down the door. Any extreme of thought can be thought of one who is tweaking.

Well, I beg to differ.

Tweaking is not tweaking as crack addicts have named it to be. Tweaking is not tweaking at all. To say that tweaking is any one of or all of these things is putting it quite mildly. It took me a long time to figure out what tweaking is, and it did not occur to me when, or while, I was smoking crack what tweaking really is. I had to do some deep thinking to figure out what tweaking is and now I know what tweaking really is.

The definition of tweaking manifested itself to me while I was writing this book. I sat down and began to think what tweaking is exactly. I can remember myself doing some of these abnormal things that you have just read about: hearing voices speaking, cars driving down the street and stopping in front of the house, at the stop sign with me so-called tweaking wondering if it was the police. There are so many ways that a person can be tweaking that it is uncountable and even more unattainable. This is getting us nowhere.

So, what is tweaking? There is only one definition for the term called tweaking and that definition is Satan. A person smoking crack comes from the natural thinking stage of life inhaling this drug called crack through the pipe into their lungs. The smoke quickly quickens itself straight to the human brain causing a dramatic change of thought to the mind. So, and...

This still is getting us nowhere. Let me make it simple. Tweaking is the spirit of Satan taking control of your heart, mind and spirit transforming your soul to an angel of darkness. When one is tweaking they are not tweaking at all; they have become possessed by the demonic evil force of Satan; the Prince of Darkness has taken control.

There is no other drug that can make a person do the things that they do when they have smoked crack cocaine. If a woman is willing to sell her daughter for prostitution for crack, if a woman is willing to sell herself as a prostitute for crack, if a woman is willing to do anything for crack, then that woman has become possessed by the spirit of Satan by smoking crack. If a man is willing to commit the act of homosexuality for crack, if a man is willing to rape even his own mother and or sister under the influence of crack, he is demonically possessed by Satan. If a man is willing to hurt anyone and do bodily harm even to himself as well as his family; if a man is willing to rob a bank, a store with a gun, real or not; if a man is willing to do anything and everything to get some more crack; if a woman is willing to do anything and everything to get some more crack—they are not tweaking, my friend. They have become possessed by the spirit of Satan. In actuality they have become Satan. They are the devil. Oh, yes, let me say this also, this tweaking stage does not last that long all the time but for the time that it does, that is exactly who these people come to be; Satan.

These cases are extreme but all of these cases, each and every one, has happened in the addiction of people who have and are strung out on crack and this is the honest to God truth. The longer you smoke crack, the more open you invite the spirit of Satan into your soul.

There is no such thing as tweaking. So, stop playing with that term (addicts) to justify a person's demonic act of sin because sin is sin in itself. Tweaking is one thing and one thing only.

A person in this state of mind called tweaking while smoking crack has literally become the devil themselves. And if you are an addict smoking crack/crank, you are worshipping Satan every time you put the rock on the screen and inhale the smoke into your lungs. You take the chance, man, woman, boy or girl, of committing the most perverted acts of sin in society that there are.

You have become Satan himself in your flesh. You are the devil. And that, my friend, is what tweaking is.

For I know that in me (that is in my flesh) dwelleth no good thing: for to will is present with me but how to perform that which is good I find not. For the good that I would I do not: but the evil which I would not, that I do. Now if I do that I would not, it is no more I that do it, but sin that dwelleth in me.

I find then a low, that when I would do good, evil is present with me. For I delight in the law of God after the inward man: But I see another law in my members, warring against the law of my mind, and bringing me into captivity to the law of sin which is in my members.

O wretched man that I am! Who shall deliver me from the body of this death? I thank God through Jesus Christ our Lord. So then with the mind I myself serve the law of God; but with the flesh the law of sin (Romans 7:18-25).

CPSIA information can be obtained at www.ICGtesting.com
Printed in the USA
268637BV00001B/31/P

Made in the USA
Columbia, SC
19 October 2024

44306519R00091